ALSO BY PAJTIM STATOVCI

My Cat Yugoslavia

Crossing

BOLLA

BOLLA

PAJTIM STATOVCI

Translated from the Finnish by
David Hackston

faber

First published in the UK in 2022
by Faber & Faber Ltd
Bloomsbury House,
74–77 Great Russell Street,
London WC1B 3DA

Published in the United States by Pantheon Books, a division of
Penguin Random House LLC, New York, and distributed in Canada by
Penguin Random House Canada Limited, Toronto.

Originally published in Finland by Kustannusosakeyhtiö Otava, Keuruu, in
2019. Copyright © 2019 by Pajtim Statovci and Kustannusosakeyhtiö Otava.

English translation copyright © 2021 by David Hackston

The right of Pajtim Statovci to be identified as author of this work
has been asserted in accordance with Section 77 of the Copyright,
Designs and Patents Act 1988

This is a work of fiction. Names, characters, places, and incidents either
are the product of the author's imagination or are used fictitiously.
Any resemblance to actual persons, living or dead, events, or locales
is entirely coincidental.

This translation has been published with the financial support of the
Finnish Literature Exchange.

The drawing on page 219 is © Pajtim Statovci and Mirella Mäkilä.

A CIP record for this book
is available from the British Library

ISBN 978–0–571–36133–5

MIX
Paper from
responsible sources
FSC® C171272
FSC
www.fsc.org

2 4 6 8 9 7 5 3 1

bolla

1. ghost, beast, fiend
2. unknown animal species, snakelike creature
3. alien, invisible

I

Having made the world, God began to regret his creation. He went to meet the Devil, who asked him, "What's wrong?"

"There's a snake in my Paradise," said God.

"Well, well," the Devil replied, barely concealing his unctuous smile. He smacked his lips and waited for God to lower his head and ask a favor, which he did next.

"Give me a child of yours and I will do as you wish, I will remove my snake from your Paradise," the Devil said, and in front of him, God was now kneeling.

"A child of mine," God repeated.

"Yes, a child of God," said the Devil, then God started thinking.

"Very well," God said eventually, forlorn. "For that, I will give you my child."

I have seen a man die, I have seen a soldier's severed hand lying in the road, it looked like a pike dug up from the earth, I have seen brothers separated at birth, houses burned to the ground and collapsed buildings, broken windows smashed crockery stolen goods, so much stuff, you'd never believe how much wreckage is left behind when life is thrashed from around it, objects die, too, when their owners are taken from them.

I've seen terrible things, terrible things after terrible things and terrible things before terrible things, bodies washed up on the shores like driftwood, horrific, sick deeds, unforgivable sins, rows of gunmen and their victims, a village of children and their parents on their knees

on the ground, and I knew that soon not one of them would be alive,
I see it like a poster in my mind, the expression that each of them bore,
the sense of impending end made their faces look empty and stiff like
the heads of porcelain dolls, they wet themselves and prayed for us not
to shoot them, and though they supported one another and gripped one
another, they touched one another as though they were strangers, men
and their wives, mothers and their children, as they pressed against one
another they pushed one another farther away, though you'd think the
opposite would happen. It surprised me that living at a moment like
that was the exact opposite of love, such a lucid awareness of death.

I have held a friend's heart in the palm of my hand, I have thrust my
hand into a chest ripped apart by bullets, grabbed a torn aorta, slippery
as an eel, felt the vertebrae of the spine like teeth against my knuckles,
rested my fingers on the lungs like wet pillows.

I have lain next to a man shot in the forest I lay next to him I
couldn't leave him, believe me all I could do was make sure he stayed
alive, and I wrapped my arms around him and pressed down on his
bandages and felt every attempt his body made to function in its
familiar rhythm, felt the murmur of his insides, his stomach hardening
as it filled with blood, felt every confused movement of every organ like
the sound of a strange animal.

Like this I lay next to a man with gunshot wounds, and many hours
passed before we were found, there in the middle of the darkened forest
they stumbled upon us, as if by a freak of nature, and they took us to a
field hospital where I operated on him, sewed up his ruptured bowels
and amputated his infected leg below the knee, and when he finally

woke up I told him what had happened in the forest and he could hardly believe he was still alive, and he gripped my hand and kissed it, and cried and said he remembered me from the forest, thank you, he said eventually, I'm eternally grateful to you, do you hear, eternally grateful for this life.

A few months later I received a letter. I had been transferred and had already forgotten about him. The letter read, You kissed me, there in the forest, didn't you, isn't that right, you kissed me on the lips, and on my neck and cheeks and forehead, you kissed me, and you touched me when you thought I was unconscious, didn't you, when you thought I was dying? Because I was so cold that your lips were fire. Isn't that right? That these memories are not dreams?

I read his letter dozens of times, but only rarely did I manage to get to the end, to the bit where he thanked me for saving his life, then said the same thing again: I am eternally grateful to you, grateful for every sunrise, for every night that I am alive in this world. And then he wrote, maybe, maybe we could meet again, do the same thing again, or something like that, I don't know, with both of us awake this time, I liked it

no

I'm sorry for

writing to you this way

I live in Belgrade

in case you want to visit sometime

I'll wait for you at the foot of the Mihailo Monument, for the next few weeks I'll sit on the white steps every Wednesday and every Saturday at noon, I'll be wearing a white shirt and black trousers, you'll surely recognize me by the empty trouser leg flapping in the wind, where once there was the leg you took from me.

That's what he wrote to me, and I never went to visit him—once I almost did because I was near Belgrade for a while, but I didn't because I couldn't kiss him again, of course not, a one-legged man, who would do such a thing, touch a broken man

A few weeks after his letter, the man's father wrote to me and told me his son had shot himself in the mouth with a pistol, and in the envelope was an invitation to the man's funeral. I stared at it for many days, took it from my pocket in the evenings and sometimes in the mornings, read a word or two. It smelled of smoke, and its sour aroma, a mixture of wet cardboard and burned plastic, became ingrained in my fingertips and made its way along my arms and from there into my mouth when I brushed my teeth, to my clothes from which I couldn't get rid of it, not even by rinsing them in vinegar water, and eventually I threw the letter away like a note from the devil, and I said to myself that I am a doctor, I am a doctor I am a surgeon I help people

After the funeral the man's father wrote to me again, and the letter read, "I know everything, you know what I mean, not even an Albanian would do that."

It was written on the same notepaper and its smell started following me everywhere, remained on my skin even after I had bathed and changed all the textiles in my apartment, it floated with me to the bakery, the operating gurney, on the journey from Belgrade via Gradnja to Kamenica. There, it turned into rain that fell torrentially for days: water filled the drains and gutters and streaked its way along the edges of the roads, drowning the flowers, the grass and moss, uprooting the traffic signs and cattle fences as it went, even cracking the asphalt, and eventually crept into the houses, burning and angry, rising

up to the knee

"I will end what my son did not: an eye for an eye, I am coming for you, you faggot."

the letter ended with these words can you believe how close I was to going

1

The first time I see him, he is crossing the street. What catches my eye is his sunken head, which hardly turns though the intersection is busy, then I notice his skinny body, which his string-like legs seem to pull behind them. His hair, parted down the center, looks like a pair of little wings, and he holds a pile of books against his chest; sometimes his other hand droops to the side, every once in a while he stuffs it in his pocket and pulls up his tight dark red velvet jeans.

I sit in the shade outside a café, and he walks toward me, the sun on his shoulders. I can make out the flicker in his eyes as he passes, the items in his pants pockets, the soft fuzz on his neck, his shaved arms. Then he walks onto the terrace and stands for a moment by a table at the other end of the nearly empty café. My cigarette burns down to the filter. He looks confused, as though he knows someone is observing him, and he yawns with his entire body, a deep inhalation that soon drowns like a faint puff of air behind the shyest fist I have ever seen, the palm lifted in front of his mouth opens out toward the road, like a slowly burgeoning flower, and only then does he place his books on the table and sit down.

It is early April, and I cannot take my eyes off him. He looks skittish and lost, as though he were living out an unpleasant dream, as though he keeps a different rhythm, different laws from those around him, and in his posture and gestures—the way he opens his books so gingerly, as though he is afraid of creasing their covers, the way he holds the pen he has taken from his pocket like a shard of broken crystal, how from time to time he presses his fingers against his temple and closes his eyes as if to give the impression of concentration, though I strongly suspect he is merely trying to refrain from looking around—there is something bare and untamed, something that speaks volumes yet remains unspoken.

I stand up and begin walking toward his table. I don't understand how I even dare talk to a Serb, but somehow I feel compelled to make better acquaintance with him.

"*Zdravo,*" I say in Serbian.

"Hi," he says in a bright voice, almost like that of my wife, his eyes fixed on the book lying open on the table, the text of which is so small and tightly typeset that I can't make out what language it's in.

"May I sit down?" I ask, and pull a chair from beneath the table.

"Sure," he replies, glances around, then nods at the chair and looks me in the eye, and I think what an extraordinarily, magnificently beautiful man he is, his irises look like a sky preparing for a storm and his trimmed stubble combines with his reddish hair, neatly combed and groomed, his torso long like a horse's, and his face perfectly proportioned, delicate and sweet. I can't remember how much time has passed since his answer, how long I have been staring at him or he at me like friends who have been separated for decades.

"I'm Arsim," I say and reach out a hand.

"Miloš," he says and grips my hand in his cold, bony fingers. "Nice to meet you." I release his hand and slide into his sad eyes, languid beneath his heavy, wrinkled eyelids.

The next hour feels more comfortable than any I have ever experienced. We order coffee, lower our voices, and when I see that his books are in English we switch languages. Though improbable, random even, it feels natural, because by speaking English we can be different people, we are no longer ourselves, we are free of this place, pages torn from a novel.

I discover that he is twenty-five, a year older than me, that he studies medicine at the University of Pristina, and that he will probably specialize in surgery, that he is from a small town called Kuršumlija on the other side of the border, thirty kilometers northeast of my hometown, Podujevo, which in turn is thirty kilometers northeast of Pristina, that in addition to his native language and English he speaks fluent German and even a smattering of Albanian.

I tell him perfectly normal things about myself too, the kind of things you would tell a new acquaintance: I tell him my age and where I come from, tell him that my father taught English and got me interested in languages and that one day I hope to work as a teacher of literature or a proofreader for a newspaper, and as I speak I can feel the glue of his eyes against my cheek, the way he scrutinizes my every movement, his back hunched, his head to one side, listening intently as though he were trying to memorize everything I said.

I tell him I study at the university too, literature, history, and

English, or that I used to study there, I don't know, and telling him this feels awkward and shameful as the university in which I enrolled years ago is no longer the same as the one where he studies, the place where we began our studies at around the same time.

After finishing our coffee, we look at each other for a while, and it feels right and real, unlike everything that Pristina has become, its streets filled with Serbian troops carrying assault rifles, tanks, and lines of military vehicles that look as though they have descended from space.

He smiles and I smile, and what we might look like right now doesn't frighten us, at all, because we were meant to meet, I think, and maybe he thinks it too, there's a reason the two of us happened upon this café at the same time.

At some point he asks the waiter for the bill, pays for my coffee, and says he has to visit the library before his next lecture.

"Do you want to come along?" he asks.

I don't need anything at the library right now, but I say of course I'll join him. We walk the short way, cross the street, and arrive at the university campus, step on the grass, whole chunks of which the years have gobbled up with gray, damp, worn stone slabs, and we climb the few steps up to the entrance to the library, which looks like it has been wrapped in a fishing net, and walk into the large, bright lobby as though into the inflamed jaws of an ancient monster. The floors are a grand marble mosaic and along the walls are round metallic roses that look on with a watchful gaze, like the eyes of the gods.

He walks slightly in front of me, and suddenly I grip him by the shoulder, as if I were a madman, a schizophrenic, there in the middle of the lobby, just like that, wholly out of character, without giving it a thought, right in the midst of the crowds of people filing out of the building, in the heart of the close, humid afternoon I really grab him, and he stops and only after a moment turns his head, looks first at my hand on his shoulder, the tips of my fingers resting on the arc of his collarbone, and then at me, and for that brief moment I am a completely different man— *so alive,* I say to myself, so much more alive than I have ever been before.

He is a Serb and I am an Albanian, and by rights we should be enemies, but now, as we touch, there is nothing between us that is strange or foreign to the other, and I have an unwavering certainty that we two, we are not like other people, and the feeling is so visceral, so bright and clear that it is as though it has come from on high, like a message addressed to us, and we don't care in the least how many people roll their eyes or ask us to move out of the way, how many snigger as they pass us, perhaps at the fact that we are unable to form words, neither to them nor to each other.

And when he eventually asks whether I'd like to see him again in the same café next week around noon, when he allows his face to break into a hint of a smile, which he instantly tries to control like an inappropriate bout of laughter, to which I respond with a smile of my own and say, *let's meet a week from today in the same café,* my life splits in two, into the life before him and the life after him, everything until this moment becoming an almost insignificant detail, surpassed like a hastily conjured white lie.

It is early April, and I desire another man so unmistakably that for the rest of the day he is with me in my prayers, in which I shamelessly ask god to give him to me.

That same evening my wife serves me a meal of bean soup, fried bell peppers dressed in cream sauce, feta cheese, tomatoes, cucumber, and *ajvar*. While I am eating, she sits down across the table, her expression worried, as though she were holding her breath or stuck in uncomfortable company.

Ajshe and I were married young, in early summer four years ago at the behest of my father, who later succumbed to liver disease. I was only twenty, the sole child in my family. My father said Ajshe was an exceptional woman, demure and obedient, intelligent despite her lack of education, skillful, well-mannered, and from a good family. I was promised there could be no wife more decent, no mother more dutiful than Ajshe.

And so, at the dying wishes of my father, I said I would take her to be my wife, as long as her father consented and promised that Ajshe would live up to the impeccable words that had been spoken about her. When Ajshe's father was assured that I was an upstanding and trustworthy young man, that I didn't believe in the fist, that I would never commit adultery, that I would never lose so much as a dinar in gambling and the bottle was no threat to me because, just like my father, I understood the value of education and was about to enroll at the university, I was granted his permission to marry her.

We wed each other for a simple reason: because it's better for people to live with someone than to live alone, because a man should have a woman by his side and because a woman should have a man by her side too, and because a man, especially a man like me, is expected to reproduce and continue the family line; it's important for a man to have at least one son to whom he can leave his house, land, and money.

Our countryside wedding was traditional, Ajshe was getting herself ready for weeks, preparing her trousseau and bidding farewell to her former life, and I started making space for her and hoped she would get along with my parents. The worst scenario would have been if Ajshe had proven stubborn, bad at taking advice, or if my mother had turned her nose up at her new daughter-in-law's ways of doing housework.

On our wedding day, she was brought to me. She was remarkably beautiful, silent as a drape, as was expected of her, her wedding dress looked like folds of pleated golden-edged silk paper sprinkled with glitter, and as I lay with her for the first time that night she breathed heavily only a couple of times, though she bled, though I could see how much pain she was in.

After showering separately, I told her that she had looked stunning all day, that I had never seen a more beautiful woman, and that I was happy she was my wife, and she said she too was happy and proud that I was her husband and the father of our future children, and we soon fell asleep; I drifted into a restless dream and she slumbered in pain.

"I promise to look after you as best I can, to be your right hand, your rock," Ajshe said the following morning as though she were reading a hymn, putting on the heart-shaped earrings I had given her as one of many wedding gifts, and in her words there wasn't the slightest worry about the future and not a trace of the discomfort of the previous evening.

My father died two months after our wedding. He had been ill for a long time, and in his final weeks he was very weak, but his death was good because he got to see me with a woman like Ajshe.

To my relief, Ajshe is exactly the kind of person I was promised. She is patient and understanding, bighearted. She's always listened and encouraged me, and she's never spoken out of turn to me or my parents, and when I told her that one day I wanted to write a book set in ancient times, a story of war, of the centuries-long humiliation of the Albanian people perhaps, the most breathtaking love story ever written, she said: "What kind of people write books if not men like you? Just tell me if there's anything I can do to help you."

She is proud of me, as though I were already a writer immortalized in books and magazines, the embodiment of my dream. She said things like this, unaware of how much time and energy such a profession required.

When my mother fell ill with cancer two years later, Ajshe took care of her; she washed her and changed her clothes, fed her, kept her company and listened to her. All the while she managed to cook dishes one more delicious than the last, even though we didn't have much money, because alongside my studies I could only do occasional shifts as a waiter at a restaurant in Pristina to make ends meet.

After my mother's death, I sold the house to my relatives and bought an apartment near the center of the city. I had to give up my car, but at least I was closer to the university and my job. I also wanted to get away from my family village, because the twisted rural pastime of spying on people and talking behind their backs has never suited my character.

We swapped our nice, large three-story detached house for a one-bedroom unit in a run-down apartment block in Ulpiana, where Ajshe is to remain quiet as a mouse whenever I need to study or write or sleep. She never protests, though I know her true desire has always been to live in a large house, somewhere peaceful where she can bring up children, have animals, and take care of the land. But wherever I go, she will follow.

Oftentimes I think how lucky I am that she is my wife and that she has precisely this kind of character, especially when I hear stories about how a woman who has entered the household has broken the peace by arguing with her in-laws, bringing shame on her husband by constantly disagreeing with him, or neglecting her duties of housekeeping and childcare.

At other times I think I don't deserve her—when we make love, for instance, when she sees how I rush then, how I pretend to ejaculate, how I avoid her touch or touching her—and I slip into dejection because I realize that I am not worthy of her, that she is far too good to be mine, to spend this life with me.

Worst of all is the knowledge that Ajshe would never tell me if she wanted to live differently. Or, no, worse still is the fact that respecting each other has turned into something of a competition, one in which I always lose.

The affection she gives me and the love she lavishes upon me—I often wonder if I will ever be able to respond to it.

That night, as we sit at the kitchen table, Ajshe says my name in a way that she has never said it before. Her voice is so quiet, so feeble that I almost know what she is about to say, and I know she is afraid of those words too.

"I am pregnant," she continues abjectly, lowers her eyes, then looks up at me again, then down again and clasps her hands on the table.

"Are you sure?" I ask and put down my spoon.

Why does the child have to come now, I wonder, why couldn't it have come earlier, back when we had enough space for it, in the years we said would be perfect for our firstborn?

"Yes," she says slowly. "I couldn't tell you sooner, I wasn't sure until I went to the doctor today. I'm sorry I did this without telling you, but I wasn't sure why my stomach has been so restless recently. The doctor told me the pregnancy is already quite advanced, though my period has continued as normal. The baby is due in July."

For a long while we look at each other in silence; making the slightest sound or movement feels wrong and inappropriate.

She is the first to look away, her eyes moving along the serving dishes, the walls, the windows, she looks at everything except me. And something happens, I can't explain what happens within me, but I stand up as though wrenched from my chair and take a few steps closer to Ajshe, who now seems emotionless, like a complete stranger.

Then, for the first time ever, I slap her with the back of my hand.

Her head jolts to the side and she lets out a hopeless whimper, and when with her eyes shut she asks for forgiveness, I learn that violence only begets more violence.

We spend the night in separate rooms. I go to bed wondering whether this could be the best and worst day of both our lives.

The following week I see him again. The morning mist lingers, stiff as a tortoise rolled on its back, what is left of winter slowly giving way to spring. Every day feels more anxious, more ominous than the previous one, and the people are increasingly restless; even the houses are on their toes.

He sits at the same table, in the same uncomfortable-looking position, with a cup of coffee, two small apples, and a pouch of juice. I walk right up and stand across from him. As soon as he notices me, he picks up one of the apples and takes a bite.

"Hi," I say and sit down.

"Hi," Miloš answers and places the bitten apple back on the table.

I order myself a macchiato, light a cigarette, and begin restlessly swinging my leg under my chair as he munches on his apple.

"How's it going?" he asks once the waiter has brought my coffee.

"Fine. You?" I say a moment later—and I realize I'm staring at his mouth.

"Fine," he replies and licks his lower lip.

We are quiet for a while, but there's nothing awkward about our silence. I commit to memory the way he leans back, the contours of his arms, the way he carries himself as he crosses his legs, his high cheekbones and his skin, like dry bread, his hips, small and round like those of a young girl, the way he speaks, meticulously and cautiously, as though he were giving careful consideration to every syllable, his white teeth, and the way his smile spreads across his angular features, wide and wrinkled like the stomach of someone sitting down.

I start talking about whatever comes to mind, my patchy sleep, the book I am currently reading, about how shortsighted, unsustainable, and damaging it is to everyone that the Serbian government has hounded Albanian teachers and students out of the university, about my part-time job in a Serb-owned restaurant not very far from here, about customers who order only a coffee and occupy the tables for hours, about how disappointed I am with President Rugova and the way he merely repeats the same things day after day, asking the Albanians to hold on, hold on, about the courses I am undertaking in all kinds of places, in Albanian-owned private apartments, empty warehouses, offices, and basements, and of how humiliating it feels, and he smiles at me empathetically as though we have known each other forever, and as he tells me more about his studies at the faculty of medicine, about his one-room apartment a few blocks from the campus, about his summer job—he works at a restaurant too—he allows his eyes to run the length of my body, uninhibited; he looks at my arms and shoulders, he looks at my neck and chest, my sides, he looks at my lips and forehead, just as I look at him, all of him, so that every moment we spend not touching each other feels stolen.

"Do you want to get out of here?" he interrupts at some point.

"Yes," I reply instantly, like a ravenous animal.

"To my place, I mean," he whispers.

"Yes," I say and stand up.

We leave the café terrace and walk out into the street, and suddenly I feel frightened, as though the entire city can hear my thoughts, as if everyone knows where we are going and why.

We pass a dressmaker's, a small newspaper kiosk inside which a teenage boy in a baseball cap is smoking a cigarette, a busy restaurant with four Serb soldiers sitting at a table outside looking smugly around, then we skip past a thrift shop, its wares spilling out across the pavement, and arrive at his apartment building, and barely has he opened the door and closed it behind us than I am all over him—there in the dark urine-smelling stairwell, scraps of paper and cigarette ends all over the floor, there against the wall mossed with ingrained dirt, I kiss him.

His lips taste sweet like fresh fruit, I note in my all-consuming desire, my eagerness to see him naked, then he pulls me behind him up the flight of stairs to his apartment, his small studio where we make love like filthy dogs, we tear the clothes from each other, he kisses me and touches me all over, and I kiss him everywhere, insatiable, without rhyme or reason; as though he were about to slip from my hands I grip his wrists, harder, as though he wasn't real, as though his body temperature wasn't absolute, I press my body against his body, tighter still, and though he gives me power over him, I wrest him off and shake him as if in a fit of rage, I sniff him and the air between us, the salty scent of his skin, and I admire his slender build, his bulging veins, his sides where his ribs shine through like yellowed strokes of a paintbrush, his smooth, freshly shaved body, and I stick a finger between his buttocks, press my tongue between them, then into his mouth too, and push his head against the pillow. His flesh yields to my commands like dough; I decide what happens to him now, and that is what he wants.

A moment later, we lie next to each other on the sweaty bed, and I feel both heavy and light as a breath, I feel guilt and happiness, the two do not cancel each other out, and I don't feel shame either, though he too looks a little hollow and bereft.

"You are so handsome," he says eventually and gives a short laugh, stands up, and reaches for his trousers, from the pocket of which he pulls out a pack of cigarettes and a lighter.

"Thank you," I say. "You are . . . too. Beautiful."

He takes a cigarette for himself, then hands me one and lights them in the same order. After the first puff I am about to ask him, almost out of habit, to start getting dressed, when he voluntarily picks up my shirt and trousers and places them in my lap, then begins putting his clothes on, the cigarette still burning between his lips.

I look at the apartment, a kitchenette just big enough for a small fridge and with little counter space; in the hallway a door standing slightly ajar leads into a bathroom with a darkened bathtub and cracked yellow tiling, and in the main room there's a sofa bed, a two-seater table, a wonky TV stand, bare white walls, and a dark blue threadbare carpet to which the sheets have fallen, still bearing our shapes.

I have slept with a man; the thought scurries at the edge of my mind. I have just slept with another man, I repeat to myself and smile, and it felt better than in my most unbridled imaginings, insane and insanely good.

I finish my cigarette, quickly pull on my clothes, and leave the apartment nodding to the question he asks from the bed, almost with a grimace, as I leave: "Want to meet tomorrow? Here, after midnight?"

As I wander around downtown, it feels as though the earth moves beneath me, slowly rising to the rhythm of my footsteps like ruins waking from a dream. I watch with surprising calm as children chase one another in front of the Boro and Ramiz Hall, kicking a ball and teasing one another, but by the time I reach the theater I am so agitated that I almost trip over my shoelaces and stumble under a bus, and I stop at the newspaper kiosk to buy a chocolate bar and some chewing gum, which I stuff into my mouth.

When I arrive home, I tell Ajshe that this is the worst possible time for a new life, and she nods in agreement.

"Yes, it is," she replies and strokes her stomach.

That night I wake to the sound of rain. A wild shower frantically whips the roads and rooftops, lapping the grit and dust from the ground and carrying it away like a gray gruel, eventually flushing it down the drains, out of sight.

27 FEBRUARY 2000

Do you ever wonder what you and I might have become, how happy we might have been in another time, another place maybe? I think about it all the time, here I have all the time in the world to think and write, to think what to write in this journal they gave me.

Some say people remain the same throughout their life, but while I've been here I've realized that turning into something else, someone else, is just child's play, the flick of a switch, all it takes is the desire to change, the ability to close your eyes, the imagination, the determination to walk unwavering through painful memories, to progress through the rising tide of past cruelties to a place where the landscape by the side of the road is new, the air thick with tomorrow.

My imaginings are lovely, they move me, because in those thoughts we are not looking backward or to the sides but at each other, and I'm so pleased, so proud of us that I could snap in two like a twig—can a person even be this happy, I ask myself then, and asking that question always means that you are close enough that I can sense you and smell you, whenever I want, you are not going anywhere and neither am I.

There I will see you again and everything will start over from the beginning, nothing that happened or didn't happen between us matters, and there will be no sense of time, no earth that will not carry us, no wars no beliefs no people to push us apart, but there will be a house and a garden near the shore, sand and young forests and level fields, and now and then the rich smell of grass will rise to our nostrils, and from the window we can see all the way to the sea and as far as it stretches.

At times I torment myself on purpose and decide to fill the landscape with the fog gathering above the sea; it looks as though it's fighting itself, and the rain pours down and all around us suddenly a storm rages unbridled, and that's when you hold yourself close to me because you are scared too, scared that the house we built together might break apart, that the squall will wrench it all away.

But then, just as the feverish sky is spluttering, I push the rain clouds aside and cut the wind with scissors, and there you are in front of me, so alive, so utterly alive right there in front of me that I can smell your dry mouth and your wet hair, and the relief in your eyes right then, that's the best part, the moment when your tension eases into an embrace, a kiss that never ends.

.   .   .

I'm trying not to wrap myself in despair here because it won't help anyone or anything, no amount of misery will make us real again. It's wrong, and that's why I'd rather live a lie than live cowed by the truth.

Some days I'm perfectly content—I'm in a good mood, lively and creative—and I try to imagine new things about us, that you have published a book about our unlikely story, with all our words just as they were meant to be, you appear and tell me all about it with a childish glee, and I have just come home from the hospital and I tell you that I already knew, I knew this about you, I knew this day would come, how talented you are, and as I lavish you with hugs I can say quietly to myself that you are mine, mine, mine forever, you are mine and nobody will take you from me.

Or I imagine you reading a book on the couch, as concentrated as always, and you don't even hear when I say something mundane, how many eggs would you like or how about I change the sheets today, you don't hear me and I find it charming, you and your books.

Or then I might imagine you arriving at the house without my noticing, feeling only when you grip me from behind and your breath covers the skin of my neck in goose bumps, then I turn and there you are, firm as a stone column and so unimaginably beautiful, like a summer flood in the heart of winter, a pristine lake in the middle of a desert, something so dazzling and curious that it's impossible to put into words, then with all that you have, you say what you once read to me from that book of yours, that you love me so much and that you're so happy that it's painful, do you remember how crumbled the love in that book was, "I love you so much it hurts" and "I'm so happy that

I can't breathe," it went something like that, I'll always remember it because there was something so mournful and comforting about it, to love someone so much that you can't breathe

can something like that really exist

But then I feel it too, like a chain saw in my stomach, a fresh bullet wound in my calf, the frost on my chest set alight.

"so much it hurts so happy that I can't even breathe"—right?

2

PRISTINA, 1995

We spend more time together than we do apart. I go to him late
in the evening. He leaves a piece of cardboard between the door
and jamb. We always exit the apartment at different times: once
we've made sure, one ear against the door, that there's nobody in
the corridor.

Though I learn more about him all the time, his daily routines
punctuated with too little sleep, his scant diet, his unwavering
concentration, his tendency to answer everything in the affirma-
tive, on some subjects he is more taciturn: he rarely talks about
his family or childhood, so I don't ask him much and don't tell
him much about myself either.

Our time together is mostly silent, and the curtains are always
closed. We never go anywhere, not even for a walk, we don't har-
bor thoughts of any kind of life outside this apartment because

such a life simply doesn't exist. We spend the days lying on his bed. I want him over and over and he wants me, and afterward he usually places his ear against my heart, and we lounge there for hours, our arms and legs entwined.

I have never felt as good or as safe as when I am with him. I have never opened any door with as much anticipation as when I do his, never waited to see anyone as eagerly as I wait for him, and even a short time apart feels agonizing and frightening; if he disappeared on his way to the store or if he wasn't at home one evening, it would be unbearable, the idea that this might come to an end, that I might lose him after such a short time together.

At times, I feel guilty and dirty about what we do, and I get nervous and don't want to see anyone, even him. I allow myself to consider that I don't really know anything about this person, he might gossip about me, take a clandestine photograph of us and make copies for everyone, or while I'm asleep he might thrust a dagger into my eye and watch me bleed to death. He could do anything, I think, but then he gets up from the table and lies down on the bed simply to give me a kiss, and in doing so he banishes all my doubts, all my questions, all my grounds for worry.

He spends his time studying diligently because he wants to become a heart surgeon one day, to actually cut people's hearts open for a living. His apartment is full of books, folders and piles of papers, lecture notes in small, barely legible handwriting with Post-it notes on top, codes and graphs, formulas and numbers that look like yet another language he speaks.

One of his textbooks, the most important one, is so massive that when it's opened it covers the entire desk. The pages are the thickest and heaviest I have ever seen, filled with pictures of cells and organs in minute detail. He stares at the book's images so close up that it sometimes looks as though he is licking them, often spending hours on a single spread. He is constantly feeling his body and comparing himself to the images; he prods his ribs and throat, runs his slender fingers along his spine, presses a hand against his groin, touches his knees, his shoulders and joints, strokes his face, temple, and neck, and sometimes he asks me to lie on the floor on my back and breathe deeply so he can explore my chest with his chilly, metallic fingers at the exact point where he would make an incision in a coronary bypass operation.

When he eventually thanks me, says that he doesn't know of anything more beautiful than the human body and that I can get up, I could almost laugh. Though I respect and even admire his determination, his patience and dedication, the thought of him as a doctor amuses me because he can barely carry his own books. What will happen, I wonder, when he has to deal with a body, someone who needs to be lifted onto a stretcher or a large man with a dislocated shoulder that needs to be jammed back into place? Has he thought about how he'll cope when he has to carry out real heart surgery?

I find it extraordinary that he moved to Pristina without knowing anybody here, that of all universities he chose this one, that someone like him, a talented linguist, would really leave Serbia and move to a region riven with violence and where people have become nothing but curses to one another.

There's a war coming, I often say, to him and my friends, and I hear other people saying the same, *there's a war coming, war is inevitable, just like in Bosnia and Croatia, possibly, probably even bloodier, it won't take long before god finally turns his back on us, and then the devil will appear, he can destroy and demolish in peace, he'll thrive on violence that nobody can remember a time living without,* that's the word on the street.

What could there possibly be in Kosovo that he couldn't find in Serbia? Surely he knew that he would get a far better education elsewhere, that it would be safer at some other university, that he could apply to study anywhere he liked—abroad, Scandinavia, or central Europe—and get a degree that would open more doors than one from here?

One evening he makes us a vegetable omelette. I've just told him the next few weeks will be busy because of my work and studies, then he flips the omelette onto a plate and runs the red-hot frying pan under the tap, where it starts hissing angrily like a viper goaded with a stick.

"Come," he says, and I get up from the bed and sit at the table. "Aren't you having any?"

"Maybe later," he says, and I've learned that this means I can eat the whole omelette if I want.

He eats so rarely and so little—and almost always only fruit, mostly apples, which he has all around the apartment, in the fridge, on the tables, the windowsill, on piles of books and papers and between them, in plastic bags hanging from the door handles—that I wonder how he manages to stay alive, how he can have even that much musculature, and where he gets his energy.

He slips into bed and grabs an apple from the bedside table, bites a chunk out of it. I eat quickly because he looks lonely lying there, staring at the ceiling and devouring the apple down to the core.

Once I lie down next to him, he places his head in the crook of my arm and starts speaking, his eyes still fixed on the ceiling, and without the slightest reservation he tells me that he never particularly liked his family, his kin, his childhood home or town.

"I moved here because I wanted to get away from Serbia," he tells me. "I've always known I'd leave one day. That might sound odd, especially to Albanians," he continues, then pauses. "But, well, you know how it is."

He runs his hand between my thighs.

"How what is?" I ask and give a brief, confused laugh, though I'm astonished that someone could speak about his own family this way. Only a Serb, I think, as they say. Only a Serb.

"This. *You know?*"

He starts caressing my testicles, and I wish he hadn't said anything at all, about his family and certainly not about us, insinuating what we are to each other, because though we are here now, though we hear the words spoken between us and feel each other's flesh, we will never be more than that. Then I roll on top of him, spread my spit into him, and we make love, rougher than usual; for the first time he asks me to slap his sides, his back, and buttocks while I'm inside him.

Afterward, as we lie close, as I listen to his heavy breathing, I think how unfair it is that there are two kinds of people in this world: people who don't need to fear anything and people who ought to fear everything. That's how fear works: it arrives all at once, and it is indivisible.

The following evening I learn that he has an older brother and a sister, who is the elder of his siblings. He tells me his brother is a pharmacist and that his sister worked as a nurse until she married, his father was a dentist until he died a few years ago, and his mother, who had died young, was a secretary in an accountant's office. According to him, the only thing he and his family share is the desire for an education.

Miloš sits on the bed and I am on the floor; he massages my shoulders, against which his fingers now feel soft and supple.

"I think they envy me," he says from behind me. "Because when I was young I wasn't very interested in studying, let alone medicine, and now they don't care about me because—" He interrupts himself as though he is about to reveal a secret, to say something he hasn't fully thought through. "Well.

"You know," he continues, letting out the air that has gathered inside him. "My hometown . . . it's so small, you know, the villages, the distances between the villages, the people from one another, everything is so small . . . Envy makes people climb the walls, empty the house . . . ," he says and stops massaging me for a moment. "Have you ever felt that kind of envy?"

"I don't think so," I reply, and I think of asking whether he has heard the stories that people here tell about the envy of the Serbs, but just as I am about to, I hold my tongue. "I'm not a very envious person."

"I had no option but to leave; I haven't missed anything about my past. This is better for me, better for them, better for everybody. I can do whatever I want, whenever I want, with whomever I want. Anyway, that's that. We never have to speak about this again," he says and taps me on the shoulder. "All right?"

"All right," I reply with a smile.

Before we turn in for the night, I go to the bathroom. On the way, I think about how cramped his apartment is, the lumpy bed covering a quarter of the floor; there isn't much furniture yet still there's too much, and the globe lamp hanging low from the ceiling is dusty and takes up space like a moon reeled into the room.

I look at myself in the battered old mirror and wash my hands, though they're not dirty, and return to him, sit on the edge of the bed.

"Is everything all right?" he asks.

"Yes. My wife is pregnant," I reply, unable to make out his expression in the dusk.

"That's okay," he says.

"My parents have passed away too," I hear myself saying.

"Really?"

He places a hand on my thigh, starts twisting my hairs between his fingers.

"Yes."

He sits up, runs his hand along my neck, whispers that he is sorry about my parents, and kisses my throat right where he knows I like it.

And when I tell him I really do want to write for a living, *stories of my own for newspapers, articles and interviews, other kinds of texts too, vignettes, short stories, maybe even novels,* and when he responds by saying, *one day you will be a writer, I'm sure of it,* I start to smile and think there's nowhere I would rather be than by his side, here.

"Say it," he insists, reaches over to open the curtains a little, letting a strip of bright light from the street shine in and illuminate his face, then sits down, his legs crossed, one foot on the bed, the other on the floor.

"Say it, then it will come true. That's how I convinced myself for years. Every morning I stood in front of the mirror and repeated, *I will be a doctor, I will be a doctor, I will be a doctor, I will be a doctor,*" he proclaims, brushes the hair from his forehead, and takes me by the hand. "I said it so many times, tens, hundreds of times every day, because I didn't believe I would become anything, and I was alone for so long that the mantra I repeated to myself every morning was the only thing that kept me alive." Then he takes a breath and looks almost panicked now, "Dreams follow the lies we tell ourselves, *I will be a doctor, I will be a doctor, I will be a doctor,* I repeated over and over and I got so excited, *I will be a doctor,* and so my lie began to come alive, and the person left outside that lie, the person I thought I was, was left further and further in the past, *I will be a doctor, I will be a doctor,* once I arrived here and enrolled at the university, *I will be a doctor.* And now I will be a doctor, can you believe it, I really will become a doctor," he booms. "One day you will become a writer and you will publish books. Say it."

"One day I . . . will be a writer," I say, and letting my dream out into the open in front of him feels so silly that it comes out in two parts.

"No," he says sternly. "I will be a writer. Say it. Say it right now," he demands, grips my hand, and gives it a reassuring squeeze.

"I will be a writer," I say again, and this time it doesn't feel at all silly or delusional; it feels like the future.

14 MAY 2000

*The nurses say I can't recover without talking. I don't understand why
I need to talk about the things I've seen, what I've done, and where
I've been. Is it because killing is supposed to put an end to everything,
corrupt everything, mark a person for life, because you can't simply kill
someone without feeling sorrow, without sinking into darkness?*

*No, that's not how it goes, I've explained to them, because in war
people die differently and kill differently than during peace, that's why
it's difficult to care about the fallen, they become statistics, nothing else,
but when I say that people look at me as though I had no compassion
whatsoever, and it both amuses and angers me—if only they knew how
quickly the mind can crack, how suddenly evil can take the place of*

good, and how easy killing is then, how simple and light, because you've managed to convince yourself that you have to kill, you have to do it now, there is no other option, you either kill someone or they will kill you, it's that simple, seamless, as immaculate as water.

Without shame I can admit that I don't feel that much guilt, except in one case: a young boy, barely a teenager, who was brought to me, beside himself with fear, shrieking in pain, in blood-soaked civilian clothes and missing his left arm, and the first thing I did was press my hand against his chest and say I know you're in pain but you're safe now I'll take care of you everything will work out—though I wanted to ask him, what are you doing here, how did a kid like you, so young, as dumb and fearless as a cow, why did you go off into battle, I was so livid I wanted to slap his stupid face and curse his wretched parents.

And he just looked at me, his eyes like molten glass, and gripped my arm with his remaining hand, and once I'd asked him his name and he'd finally managed to tell me, I raised my hand into the air, Albanian, I told everyone, this boy's an Albanian, I shouted it out, then the nurses raised their hands into the air and the boy remained where he was, lying on his sickbed, can you imagine how wrong it felt to touch him once we realized he was just a petty little Albanian, a louse.

War is born of war and there is no war that will end a war, and the disgust the boy caused was war's finger, a fist shoved down the throat, choose your side and remember that the enemy is not human, the enemy doesn't have a face, a family, the enemy is nobody's child, nobody's parent, the enemy doesn't have a sister or a brother, and the enemy doesn't feel pity and neither should you.

War is filthy and unhygienic, and nobody talks about how much dirt it causes, about the amount of equipment to be maintained, clothes to be washed and mended, wounds to be disinfected, sheets, tent fabric, surgical implements, hospital machines, disposable packaging, bandages, syringes, drip tubes, and the like—endless sacks, trucks, dumps full of rubbish, and nobody ever washes, many times I almost fainted from the smell of the soldiers' feet as I took off their boots, it was repulsive, and as I pulled off their clothes the most revolting smell rose from their groins, a fug so pungent it stopped you in your tracks, the stench of urine and excrement mixed with the rusty smell of dried blood, the singe of gunpowder and the stink of ancient sweat—a filthy man is so entirely repellent.

But once we had all retreated from around him as though from a contagious dish, it was strange to note how this Albanian boy suddenly stopped shouting, just like that, as though he no longer felt any pain though we hadn't yet had a chance to sedate him, as though he didn't want us to touch him, so profoundly did the war's spirit reside in every cell of his body, and then his eyelids closed, his legs went limp and his one arm too, short sputters sucked the last remnants of his strength, and he looked very peaceful as he died—like a slowly turning whale in its mansion in the sea.

3

I don't want to go to work. I know I should be grateful to have
a job in the first place, when most people I know do not, but my
shifts drag on endlessly because I'm thinking about him all the
time, and I realize I can barely envisage any kind of life in which
he does not play a part, and I notice the same about him too—
in the way he kisses me at every opportunity, in how passionately
he grips my waist, my ass and neck, how hard he tries to please
me by getting out of bed quietly in the mornings, by leaving gar-
lic out of the food he cooks, washing my laundry, skipping class
so he can spend more time with me.

I practically live at his apartment. Sometimes we study
together, he at the table and me lying on the bed making plot
summaries of the books I've read, writing reports and analyses.
At times it feels pointless and frustrating because I have no idea

whether the degree I'm supposed to get will have any value due to the university's ban on Albanian students. A university exists exclusively for Albanians, also called the University of Pristina, and its operations are partially funded by Albanians who have moved abroad, but still there isn't even enough money to cover the bare minimum. Science students don't have access to the facilities and laboratories that they need. What kind of doctors or technicians will they become? Some say that those responsible for the funds provided by the Albanian diaspora are involved in embezzling the money, while others say there is simply less money than is needed.

In the evenings I read him extracts from my favorite books and my assignments. It becomes a habit of ours; he sits on the bed with his back against the wall or rests his head on my chest, sometimes he chuckles at the absurdity of the events, grunts something about the characters' stupidity, and when tragedy swells, he will even comment out loud, something like *oh my god* or *that's just terrible* or *it's so unfair sometimes*. He enjoys stories with an element of the supernatural, events that don't adhere to the laws of the real world, characters and creatures that defy logical explanation.

Sometimes we listen to the radio. A goldsmith's store was burgled, a kiosk owner was fined because he was unable to sell Serbian soldiers a particular brand of cigarettes, Albanian teachers secretly going about their jobs have been arrested again, and the Serbs have cut off the electricity supply to Albanian-populated areas. We can only keep the radio on for a short time because it never tells us any good news. We don't know which news stories to believe, what has actually happened and what people only say has happened. We are hidden from view like a set of keys in a pocket, and we follow the rapidly emptying city from behind closed curtains.

We hear that at one of the numerous protests a student was hit

over the head with a shovel, and when sometime later someone
claims he died in the hospital from his injuries, I say what else,
what else will they come up with to kick us, what, then Miloš
opens the curtains and props the window ajar, letting the lights
and sounds of the outside world flood in, almost violently, and
says he is sorry, as though he feels guilty because the shovel was
in a Serbian hand, but it's not your fault, I tell him.

"Still," he responds. "You know."

I go home sporadically. Ajshe is always there and the apartment
looks uninhabited; she has hidden our things in cupboards,
washed the floors and walls and rugs, and dusted all the surfaces,
but still the air inside feels like standing beneath a cloak of lead.
When I arrive, she is usually knitting quietly on the living-room
couch or ironing on the floor, but when I step farther inside the
apartment she always stands up, and I can't help but look at her
unbearably swelling stomach, her belly button protruding like a
bulging eye.

I try to be quick about my business and to say as little as possible, though she never asks where I've spent the last few nights,
weeks, asking instead about my studies and work while I hur-
riedly pack clothes into a plastic bag, or she might try to start a
conversation about the price of food, the unemployment in the
Albanian community, the Serbs' megalomaniacal behavior, or
how the sound of violent shouting carries into the apartment at
night, how more and more people have moved abroad.

"People are afraid," she says and places her right hand on her
stomach. "At a time like this it's best not to make a fuss, it's best
to stay home and only go outside if it's absolutely necessary. Isn't
that right?"

"Yes," I reply. "Yes, as an Albanian that's probably best, you're
absolutely right."

"Well, bye then," she has a habit of saying once I've put my shoes on and started getting ready to leave, and every time as I open the door: "I know you're busy, but . . ."

"I know, I know, I know," I interrupt her. "See you soon," I say and hand her a little money, and when she sees it she says she can survive on less but takes it all the same and stuffs it in her bra.

That's what life is like between us now. She wants to talk, to be together, to wait together for the birth of this child, and all I can say is, *I know, I know, everything in its own time, you don't have to worry, everything will work out,* I assure her and open the door, and just before it closes I cast her a cold glance. If only she could hear my thoughts, my solemn wish that she didn't exist.

I finish the final courses of the semester with excellent grades, but I'm not proud of myself because all my classmates get the same results, as the teachers don't want anyone to drop out. I also learn that the restaurant can't offer me any extra shifts during the summer—apparently due to "changed circumstances." Though my financial situation is bad, the matter doesn't really bother me because I decide to use this extra free time for reading and writing in earnest.

As June arrives, Miloš and I don't see each other as often as before; his days are long and he gives me a spare set of keys to his apartment. He returns home in the early hours, tired and smelling of cooking fat and unable to stay awake for long. We don't even have time to properly catch up either, but I know that before long, whether it's at two or five a.m., he will always come back to me.

Besides the fact that the continual work has both a mental and physical impact on him, he always dutifully gets up early in the morning and contentedly lies down next to me at night, drained from his day but still grateful. Perhaps he is able to work so end-lessly because the moment he wakes up he assumes a particular mode of being, the dignified manner in which he speaks to him-self and with which others should speak of him. *I will be a doctor, I will be a doctor, I will be a doctor*—sometimes I wish I could talk about myself with such confidence too.

But the more I read and write, the worse a writer I become in my own eyes, and the dumber a reader too, and many of the stories that are supposed to change a reader's view of the world feel impenetrable to me, my concentration span seems nonexis-tent. I feel anxious at the sight of thick novels and their sprawling galleries of characters, at the way I can spend hours with a book, turning its pages and looking at the words but not really reading, because I don't really see them and I don't notice or pay attention to which sentences, which events are interrupted as I turn the page. The allure of reading is gone.

There are days when I am filled with certainty that the story I am sketching, the kind of story he might like too, will one day be finished, and I imagine the moment when I can read it to him and even the day my published book arrives in the mail and I can finally hold it, flick through its pages, run my fingers along the cover bearing my name, and give copies to people. How wonder-ful a feeling that must be for a writer, I imagine, to see all those years of work, all that time spent doubting, challenging, disci-plining, and punishing yourself, an entire universe in a form at once small yet vast, modest yet grand, as proof of something so significant that all that suffering finally feels worth it.

At times like that I truly believe that reality follows the lies we tell ourselves. If a surgeon doesn't assure himself he can operate on a brain tumor, will he be able to drill into someone's skull? If a young couple expecting a baby don't convince themselves that they are capable of bringing up their firstborn, what kind of future will await them and their child?

But other days I spend frustrated, incapable of moving forward—I feel silly and childish and despise myself, because everything I write lacks sense, and what only a short while ago I thought was lofty and immense is in fact pitifully small, and as I correct my mistakes I notice myself making even more mistakes; I realize I am terrible with words and nobody will ever publish anything I write.

There's nothing great about writing per se; on the contrary, it's painful and agonizing, forcing yourself to say things that others have already said far better and more eloquently. I didn't know that something I thought I loved unreservedly could feel so wrong and unpleasant. The endless need for comparison and an uncontrollable, paralyzing shame come to afflict literature once you transition from reader to storyteller—one would be better off without it.

That's how it is, really, I tell myself and wash my hands, and after returning to bed, fatigued and distant, I begin listing facts about myself: I am an Albanian in a world run by Serbs; my parents have died and everything they left to me I have sold; I am married, a husband and soon-to-be father; I study in order to enter a profession that I probably can't achieve, and I regret not studying something more sensible, law or economics, it would have made everything so much easier. I regret getting married, I regret getting Ajshe pregnant, and I regret not leaving Pristina years ago when a friend of mine suggested it.

Because no matter what you say to yourself or no matter how steadfast your self-belief, even if you are blessed with an army of will and the courage to be as unscrupulous as a politician during an election, even if you manage to convince yourself that you have it all, isn't the most probable outcome that you still won't get what you want? Why should I be the exception? If everybody got what they wanted, would there even be a word to describe desire?

Over the following weeks I manage to write only a few pages, though I work on something every day, from morning till night, trying to formulate ideas for different articles and stories.

"That's really good for just a few weeks," says Miloš when on one of his rare free evenings I tell him I have finally completed a story, that I wrote it first in Albanian then translated it into English. "I'm really proud of you," he continues. "Will you read it to me?"

His request makes me feel ill, but I quickly cave because this is what I've been waiting for. What else is writing, I wonder, if not agreeing to everything, hurting yourself, tolerating your own imperfection, walking naked through a crowded square?

And so I begin:

The Girl and It

For almost a year it hasn't felt sunlight on its skin, only the cold walls of its cave, which it scratches and gnaws incessantly, nervous and restless, its claws and teeth ground and blunt; it cannot distinguish night from day, sleep from wake, its wings from the pitch darkness, or its calloused body from the stones and boulders with which from force of habit it exchanges pleasantries.

They tell its story in grim tales that frighten little children. Finish your dinner, it loves leftovers, they say, it will think you are its friend, and while you are asleep it will steal in like a breeze through the window or rise up like steam through the floorboards, so slowly

*that you won't even notice, it will climb into your bed and quietly lie
down next to you, then it will press its forked tongue in through your
nostrils, your mouth, and your ears and out through your eyes, and
with that you will die and won't live to see the following morning.
Don't talk back to your parents, don't be selfish, vain, lazy, greedy,
envious, don't lie, because it will appear and eat you alive, swallow
you like a marshmallow.*

*It lives in the judgments that the enraged hand down to one
another, the words used to describe the stubborn and the agitated, the
resentful and bitter, and it lurks on the paths we tread alone, where
the rivers meet and the current is at its most treacherous, in abandoned houses, uninhabited forests and dales, on lonely mountains
whose tall, icy summits pierce the clouds like balloons.*

*For one day a year it is allowed out of its cave, always in the
springtime, at sunrise, when the trees stand straight and the fields
have begun to grow new hide. On that day it has a set of borrowed
wings, and it is called a* kulshedra, *but on all other days it has a
different name. It is said that while it is free it destroys everything
it sees, that it strikes the woods ablaze, emptying the towns, raz-
ing everything the people have created in the preceding year. After
this, it begins looking for somewhere suitable to nap; it visits the
sea, the land, and the heavens, and after finding an agreeable place it
sometimes forgets where it has come from, where it resided only a day
earlier, how many people it has just killed, the guilty and the guilt-
less, and even sings in a voice hoarse with allure.*

*One year, as it rocked carefree on a branch, it felt a pebble strike its
side. It boomed like thunder and disappeared from sight in the blink
of an eye.*

*"Who is there?" came a bright voice from the mouth of a girl
wrapped in a bearskin standing at the foot of the tree.*

In a flash, it darted down from the sky and grabbed the girl, wrapped itself around her body, and held her face close to its own, ran its tongue across her eye sockets, which were as empty as the pockets of the dead.

"Do you know what I am, you silly little girl?" it asked.

"No," the girl replied and began to giggle. "I am blind."

"That tickled me, by the way," she said and continued chuckling. "You are very strong," she said as it tightened its grip. "I wish I was too."

"Aren't you afraid of me?" it asked.

"Afraid?"

"Yes."

"Of course I'm not afraid of you," the girl replied, playfully tapped its hide, unable to appreciate its immensity, and laughed again. "And it's not very polite to call me silly when we don't yet know each other. I might be blind, but I'm very clever."

"Really?"

"Yesss!"

All it could do was join her chuckling; it lowered the girl to the ground, and when it was about to leave, the girl reached out her left hand and grabbed it by the end of the tail.

"Where do you think you're going?"

"Away," it replied, wriggled free of the girl's grip, and twisted into an attacking position, its hide covered in gleaming scales and crinkles, its mouth like a loaded weapon, ready to bite the girl's arm off as punishment for her impudence.

"Very well," she said. "But don't go just yet. Do you want to play with me first?"

"Play?"

"Yesss!"

After giving this a moment's thought, it agreed to the girl's suggestion, and the two of them chased each other across the fields and

*meadows, taking turns hiding in the thickets and the boughs of trees,
and as evening fell they were both exhausted and had told each other
everything—the girl about her family, who had thrown her out of
their home, because what could they do with a blind child, and it had
told her about the cave where it had lived its life and all the different
names it had been given.*

*The girl's name was Drita, which meant light, and it thought the
name was amusing because the girl had never seen the light.*

*Before saying goodbye, they agreed to meet again in a year's time,
and from that moment on they met every year, always in the bloom
of spring, in the same forest where they first encountered each other,
on the same path where the girl almost lost her arm.*

*Over the years, it taught the girl to hunt, to stake out prey, and to
throw a spear. It bit off one of the girl's breasts too, the better for her
to shoot a bow and arrow, and proudly followed her development into
an adult, a woman every bit as strong as a man.*

*One spring, it plucked up the courage to ask, timid and bash-
ful, if Drita would become its wife, if she could imagine them living
together, spending time together every day of the year.*

*Drita began to weep, and for a moment she was unable to answer,
so overcome she was with emotion.*

"And does it matter that I was once . . . a girl, too?" it asked.

*"No," Drita answered, catching her breath and raising her hands
to its cheeks. "It doesn't matter at all," she continued and pressed her
lips against its mouth, which was as rough as bark. "I will be your
wife, of course I will. I have seen it now."*

"What have you seen?" it asked.

"The light."

*And it is said that there they remain to this day, just the two of
them, curtsied statuesque in front of each other, in a cave on the side
of the mountain where night never retreats.*

I stumble over the words, my voice trembles, and I have to read slowly, pausing in all the wrong places, because I constantly want to change my mode of expression, to focus and correct myself, to make sure he understands all the meanings beyond the text.

But once I get going, I notice that he's listening intently, his eyes closed, and it feels as though my story is coming to life beneath his eyelids.

When I finish, he is quiet for so long that I wonder whether he has drifted off to sleep, and in the course of that silence I think of my father, who in my childhood told me a variation of the same story of which there is only a bare bone left in my story, I think of what an inordinate amount of time Miloš and I spend lying still, and I think of the times to come, what if the Kosovo Liberation Army starts forcibly conscripting people to their ranks or if the Serbs turn up to arrest me claiming I stuffed a customer's change in my pocket? What would happen then?

I listen to the wind pinching at the window frames and the quieting breathing beside me.

"Well?"

"I love it," Miloš says eventually and opens his watery eyes. "My goodness, I love it so much," he adds in front of the sweating window. "How I love it," he repeats, as though he thinks I don't believe him, though I trust that he means what he says. "Would you read it to me again, Arsim?" he then asks. "You could submit it for publication in an international magazine."

I read the story again, and after that I read it again, and each time he interprets it differently, always approaching it from another angle. He says he has heard about "it" somewhere before, in a context in which "it" is used as a warning, a rebuke, a nightmare.

"It's a snake, isn't it?" he asks.

"I suppose it is."

"A snake."

"Yes."

"But it has wings and it can talk?"

"Yes."

"Is it blind too?" he asks.

"Well, I don't know," I say.

"What do you think they do there?"

"Where?"

"In the cave. Are they still there?"

"I don't know," I reply, amused. "It's just a story I came up with."

"Yes, but still. What do they do there?"

"They live together, I suppose."

After I say this, he closes his eyes.

"Forever?"

"Yes."

"Imagine," he says. "A snake with a woman for a wife." He smiles and kisses me on the cheek. "A home that two women share," he adds, his eyes still closed.

For some reason, he starts to get on my nerves. I return my story to the desk and wish him good night on my way back to bed, and I am about to fall asleep when suddenly he starts talking, animated, as though everything he says comes into his head on the spur of the moment. He tells me he heard a similar story years ago, a story where a snake is in fact the daughter of god in disguise and not a real snake at all and where god and the devil barter using their children: a blind girl and a viper.

"Oh?" I ask.

"Yesss!" he replies and removes his hand from my chest.

"Surely not?"

I notice I find it hard to conceal my annoyance. How dare someone say something like that out loud, I think, mention god and the devil in a room like this, after everything we have done.

"Don't you talk like that," I say crudely.

"What do you mean?"

"About religion."

"Oh?"

"You can't possibly know what's on the other side."

"No, I can't," he says in self-defense. "Besides, I'm not particularly relig—"

"Then don't talk about things you know nothing about."

"Sorry," he says, startled, and places his hand above my heart. "I didn't mean to offend you, I really did like your story, I just wanted to tell you what I've heard," he continues calmly, and I feel like asking whether he understands that there are some things it's just not appropriate to talk about, that anything can and should happen in books, that a writer has the right to create an entire country at will, to rewrite history, and as he falls asleep next to me, for the first time I feel uneasy being near him.

Ajshe gives birth later that month. The child arrives early and I am not with her when it happens, though I promised I would support her through the final stages of the pregnancy and take her to a midwife we know to give birth. But after going into labor, Ajshe gets the bus to a hospital where most of the staff are Serbs. We've heard rumors that they sterilize Albanian women during childbirth.

After seeing the note Ajshe left for me on the table, I head to the hospital. Ajshe looks tired but happy, not at all frightened, and the child, a boy who, though swollen looking and two and a half kilos in weight, still looks impossibly small, is sleeping in her arms, swaddled in a blanket. The delivery went well, and the staff seem decent.

When Ajshe asks if I'd like to hold the child, I say yes and take him in my arms. I know that holding your newborn baby is supposed to feel unforgettable, momentous, and it does, undeniably so, but perhaps for different reasons than for those who told me about it.

A few days later I fetch Ajshe from the hospital. Once back home, she places the baby in a crib, erected in the middle of the living room, that her sister has given us.

"I'm happy," she says and looks at the child, beaming. "He is so beautiful. Isn't he beautiful, Arsim?"

"The baby is beautiful," I say. "It will change our lives."

Then I tell her I have decided to name the boy Driton, and Ajshe smiles at me all the more.

"Driton," she says. "Light."

They wake us up at six in the morning. After washing in a bathroom riddled with mildew and brushing our teeth with a toothbrush the size of a pinkie, we stand in line in a corridor leading to the canteen, we are handed the medicines we have been prescribed from a small hatch, and the nurses make sure we take them, then we are forced to sit down at tables bolted to the floor; the benches attached to the table legs look like human shoulders. One at a time we fetch white plastic trays and white disposable cutlery, cups, and plates—everything here is white.

Each day we are given food that tastes the same, ready and rationed on the plate, wheat bread and thick corn porridge, bland soup and sour

milk; it's revolting, devoid of nutrition, stodgy, and barely good enough
for dogs. And we have to finish everything, otherwise the nurses think
you're being insubordinate, they note down our every meal, every
movement; every expression of dissatisfaction pushes further into
the future the day you might walk out of the door through which they
forcibly brought us, as though smuggling us underground. To them we
are not even patients, we are numbers.

My ward is the one people want to be in, if they have to be here
at all, because this is where they bring the "healthiest patients," so
I've heard. In here we have doctors, lawyers, bosses, and military
commanders all together, apparently. Sometimes knowing this makes
me think that things aren't as bad as I'd thought and that there's still
hope of getting out.

We are allowed to write to our friends and families, who are even
permitted to visit us, we exercise outside for an hour at a time, and at
least to some extent we enjoy the respect of the staff because we have
access to a small TV room with board games and a modest bookshelf;
we can even request particular books and magazines, though none of
our requests have yet been met.

I think you would like that bookshelf.

Oftentimes I can't help thinking about the others; I've heard there
are children here who have spent most of their lives in cots, that a
roomful of people are washed at once using a hose, they are herded into
the bathroom where they are sprayed with cold water, and they are
mistreated all day long, locked in their rooms for days at a time, taking
turns to lie on the few mattresses provided.

Can you imagine? Not even rats deserve to live this way. What kind of person can do that or enable it by their silence?

I am becoming a horrible sight here. I don't look like myself at all. I try to avoid mirrors and reflections because what looks back at me is a . . . beast. Growing old is so grotesque, and anyone who thinks otherwise never properly lived their youth.

You'd probably say what nonsense is this, you are beautiful, extraordinarily beautiful just the way you are, and I'd say don't say that, I am terribly terribly ugly, and gaunt too, well, I am unpleasant in any case, I don't look anything like what I did the last time we saw each other, because we do nothing here but follow the passing of time.

Loneliness peels you out of your skin, cuts out your tongue, and abandons you in a stale, locked room to slowly evaporate.

4

The days become more difficult, the baby cries incessantly and struggles to suckle properly. I don't know how you are supposed to lift him from the crib or the floor, how strongly I should grip him by the arms or legs when I'm changing his clothes. The baby is hopelessly small, and its guinea pig body covered in downy hairs makes it look sickly, like a different species of human.

The longer we live with the child, the more space it seems to take up, and the more strongly I feel that there's something impudent and disdainful about its way of being; it wails night and day and never seems to sleep. And the scant time it spends asleep isn't at all fruitful or relaxing but filled with the perpetual worry that it'll soon wake up and everything will start again, this grinding reality that we call parenthood. When I was waiting for it to be born, I wasn't prepared in the slightest for how much more arduous and frightening—and not at all easier, as I had imagined—everything would be once it had come into the world.

Ajshe looks after the boy most of the time, washes him, holds him while she is cooking, kissing him as though enthralled with every sound and movement he makes. She is confident and assures me that the boy only has colic; apparently her sister's children had it too.

"You do believe me, Arsim, don't you? This is only a phase," she says, the boy sitting on her arm, looking in his eyes as though she could see the child's bright, brave future on their surface.

What Ajshe tells me about the boy is immaterial to me, and I begin to loathe the sound of him. I try to avoid the child, and I believe he must sense my reluctance as he starts crying every time I have to pick him up. What if I never learn to love this child the way Ajshe does, I wonder when I am alone with him. Mostly I just dangle a toy in front of him, anything that makes a louder noise than he does.

I begin to think there's something obscene about parenthood, especially if a child is born like this one. Out of habit.

I confess to Ajshe that from the day he was born I've wished we never had him because the boy couldn't be further removed from his name. Ajshe says she is sorry I feel this way, it will pass, she continues, and dutifully looks after the boy by herself as best she can, stays up with him all night, changes his diapers, clothes, and sheets, and eventually she stops asking for my help altogether.

The Serbian troops move around sporadically, like a forest fire, ruthlessly occupying entire areas at a time, sowing terror as they go. Life has turned cruel, and people have become used to it, a dead human body is no longer a dead human body but an image of a dead human body. Raped women, murdered men, and abused children are no longer raped women, murdered men, and abused children but merely stories of such atrocities, and the invasions and skirmishes seem to grow increasingly inhumane the more people become inured to the bloodshed.

Everybody knows that war will soon be declared here too. Conversations are no longer about the possibility of war but about when it will happen. Some people, including several of our neighbors, think the war has already begun, entire towns in Kosovo have already been occupied, and tens upon tens of thousands of Albanians have fled abroad, to Germany, Italy, France, and all across Europe, some even as far as Australia and the United States. Others say that until war is officially declared, there is no war.

Miloš is constantly apologizing to me for things that have nothing at all to do with him, acts fueled by a rabid hunger for power and not by anything in him. He even commiserates with me when I tell him that some of my classmates have turned their backs on me because I have the gall to question out loud the quality of our courses; they say this makes me complicit in the subjugation of the Albanian people, apparently it means I accept what's been happening to the university, they can't believe that I could speak about my own people, my own blood, in such unpatriotic terms, and there is no point in arguing with them, trying to explain that my education and maintaining my language skills means a lot to me, because they are deaf with rage.

Miloš is busier all the time, and I see him more infrequently because he is always taking on extra shifts: he is working full-time at one restaurant and part-time at another, while at a third he does night and weekend shifts too.

"I have to save money," he explains, and I understand him perfectly well, I would do the same in his position. "There's just so much to read that it's impossible to work long hours during the term."

I am forced to ask my brother-in-law Besnik for a loan. It is the most shameful thing imaginable, but there are no other options because while Ajshe and I can tolerate hunger and even cold, our child doesn't know what it means to go without, it only understands its own needs; in that regard children are uncompromising.

Besnik works at a factory and lives in a two-story house in the countryside, away from the maelstrom of Pristina, and when we visit them Ajshe's sister asks her about the boy and how he is doing, the birth, asks what Ajshe was thinking giving birth in a hospital, risking handing such a beautiful boy over to the clutches of the Serbian nurses, and at some point that evening, once we have eaten, Besnik leads me out to the patio behind their house and suggests, for the umpteenth time, that I take a job at the factory.

Ajshe has told me that Besnik pities me because I don't have any brothers, but I don't understand why, because that's the way it has always been. Can you really miss something you've never had?

"It wouldn't be so bad, would it?" he says from beneath his thick eyebrows as we sit smoking, his black hair, heavy with gel, cascading across his neck. "You and Ajshe could live at our house, you can have one of the rooms upstairs," he continues and places a hairy hand, marked by cuts, on my thigh.

"Or we could start thinking about moving abroad," he says and squeezes my thigh. "What do you think?"

I politely refuse his suggestion, saying I greatly appreciate the gesture because we are not even close family, we don't owe each other anything, I slip the money he gives me—a thousand German marks—into my pocket and give him my word that I'll pay him back with interest.

"I promise you, my brother," I say and move his hand away.

On the way back to Pristina, I start to feel sick sitting at the back of the bus, the baby is crying and wets itself, Ajshe changes its diaper in her lap, and as soon as she is finished the baby decides to empty its bowels, and it smells so repulsive that for a moment I wonder whether I should simply disappear with the money and never come back.

I don't say a word to Miloš about my financial predicament, though he guesses as much—from the amount I eat at his apartment, from the fact I've had to give up smoking and wear the same clothes for days at a time, from how bad I smell because I can't be bothered to wash. He knows that my situation and my future prospects look hopeless, that the only thing keeping me here is him.

At the beginning of July, he surprises me by telling me he has bought us bus tickets to Ulcinj. He presses the tickets into my hand and says: "I've taken care of everything, I've saved up for this, this is my present to you, Arsim, these four days at the beach, I couldn't get any more time off, we met three months ago and we still haven't celebrated it at all. We deserve this."

Then he smiles at me so beautifully that saying no doesn't even cross my mind.

The following week we board a packed bus, and getting to our destination takes a long time because for most of the journey the roads are not paved, just thin dirt tracks, narrow and full of potholes, running along the mountainsides, and at every sharp turn it's as though the driver is playing with our lives, barely braking, though there's no way he can see if anyone is coming toward us.

At the Kosovo-Montenegro border, Serbian officials storm the vehicle, stare suspiciously at the passengers, handguns hanging from their belts; they open up people's bags and suitcases, ask all the Albanians to empty their pockets and show their wallets, all this before telling me I won't be allowed into Montenegro because I don't have official permission to cross the border or written proof of the purpose of my journey, a document I've never heard of before. I am so nervous that my tongue feels paralyzed, but when Miloš hands both guards some money, his fingers trembling, and says something so quickly that I can't make it out, they step off the bus and wave us through the checkpoint.

And so the journey continues; we sit in the back seat, I take a tissue, wipe my sweaty brow, and try to read a book, while Miloš stares curiously out of the window at the swollen stomachs of the mountains and their colorful, undulating valleys.

As we approach our destination, Miloš has the nerve to slide his left hand between my legs, then he closes his eyes, breathes deeply, and rests his head against my shoulder, like it is just the two of us, and I push his hand away, wondering when the trip in this swelteringly hot bus with no toilet will end, whether it ever will. Doesn't he understand that if someone had seen him touch me like that, it would be the end of us?

Finally we arrive at Ulcinj, a small, picturesque town populated mainly by Albanians that attracts tourists from across the Balkans and beyond and whose long beach, Plazhi i Madh, stretches for twelve kilometers. We stay at one of the largest beachfront hotels, and every day is like the day before: we wake up early, eat a hearty breakfast and cross the street, rent a parasol, place it in the sand and sunbathe for as long as there's sun, and at some point in the day we buy ice cream from the vendors walking up and down the beach, most of whom are young boys, just kids, and we fetch afternoon coffee too. As evening draws in, we dress up smart and have dinner at a local restaurant, then return to the hotel room and curl up against each other though our skin still stings from the sun.

In Ulcinj's old town there is a castle built by the ancient Illyrians and Greeks of antiquity. On the final day of the trip, we visit the hilltop castle, where some children claim in a fanciful voice that they can see all the way to Italy, though all my eyes can spot is water.

There's no war here, I think at the top of the hill as I look out at the melancholy sea, the war is somewhere else, and when I look at Miloš in his white T-shirt, brown trunks, and dark blue sunglasses, I am not the same man I was in Kosovo; there is no room in my world for anything but these days spent here and him: how he subtly asks for the bill and pays it, how he slips packs of cigarettes into my pocket, how feverishly he looks at me when we awake to the morning light, so bright that it snatches away the tiredness we feel from our restless dreams, how he steps out of the water and looks around for a moment, almost in panic, because he can't immediately place me among the crowds on the beach, how adorable he looks when he eventually finds me and can push his fears aside because I am exactly where he left me and haven't disappeared.

"I don't want to leave," he says on our final evening, fetches us two cold beers, and walks out to the balcony in our hotel room, and leaning against the railings he gazes out at the traffic along the beachfront boulevard, the streams of people, and the sky washed in the city lights, looking like an old blackboard.

"Me neither," I say, go to him, and put an arm around him.

"Are you happy?" he asks across the railing, somewhat out of the blue.

"I don't know."

"I don't know either. But I'm not sure I've ever met someone who is truly happy."

"Right."

"But I am happy, at least sometimes, I'll admit that," he says and turns to look at me.

"Me too. It's something."

"It is something," he repeats with a curt smile and gives me a weary look.

"It's quite a lot, actually," I say.

Miloš's eyes appear to gleam, and I stroke his lower back.

"Maybe happiness is knowing that happiness doesn't exist," he says eventually. "And sorrow is the wisdom to endure it," he continues and turns to look out to sea. "I've been thinking about the last book you read . . . The way that every character was searching for happiness and all of them eventually found it," he adds and touches his hair. "They actually . . . made me angry, though I told you I liked the book, and I'm sure I did like it a bit."

"Really?"

"Yes . . . It was as if they thought that every moment they were unhappy was time wasted, as if happiness was their incontrovertible destiny, you know? That's not how it goes, at least I don't think so."

"Yes," I reply. "I don't think so either."

"Most people aren't like that."

"No, they're not."

"You see it every day. It's easier to submit to tyranny than it is to fight against it. That requires so much more," he says and exhales a long breath as though through a straw.

"I . . . I like you very much," I stammer and remove my hand from under his T-shirt.

Again he turns to look at me, squints, and grips my hand.

"I like you too. A lot."

This is the most perfect day of my life, I think, and the happiness we feel that evening, we both know it, the sensation as I kiss his neck, the person I am as I smell his hair, the gazes we cast upon each other, the taste of beer left on the balcony table, the way our lips touch right there in the flames of the fading evening, it will never end, even if there's nothing left of it by morning.

5 NOVEMBER 2000

Those months that we knew each other they were the best of my life, untainted, because we didn't have to explain anything to each other, anything at all, we were floating in space, bathing in the eternal morning like two sundials.

5

On the bus to Pristina, Miloš tells me that once we get back I'll see him even less than before.

For some reason, I begin to feel awkward being in his apartment when he is not there, though I know I can be there whenever I want. But I can't concentrate at his place the same way I did before. I am easily distracted by sudden noises carrying in from the corridor, the rhythms of footsteps in the stairwell, the banging of doors opening and closing, the clink of keys turning in the lock; all I can do is wait for the door to open and for him to step inside.

A few days after our return, Ratko Mladić and his troops murder thousands of people in Srebrenica, randomly opening fire at unarmed civilians.

The ensuing days are sheer insanity, the streets filled with a sense of perdition. People say the Serbs forced children to watch their parents and siblings bleed to death, that pregnant women had their stomach slashed open, letting their unborn children ooze out of them like sludge.

"Imagine," I say to Miloš. "That someone can do something so terrible, so repulsive to another human being."

"I know," he says mournfully. "I'm sorry."

The news knocks the wind out of my lungs; even loose sweaters feel like straitjackets, and eating, sleeping, washing, even changing clothes requires unreasonable amounts of effort. Talking about the war feels disrespectful, like the desecration of the dead; it's as though you don't have permission to talk about anything, neither the Serbs' brutality nor their momentary defeats. I feel even more miserable at the news that the Croatian army has recaptured Krajina and finally driven the Serbs out of the city in a refugee convoy—only then to bomb it.

The destruction raging around us becomes a secret; talking about it gives it a face, while remaining silent gobbles up the rest of summer like a fistful of air.

As the new term is about to begin, Ajshe tells me she is expecting another child. She says it in passing, as if this were just another everyday event, as if she doesn't care about my opinion in the least, and walks into the living room, possessively picks up the boy, and sits down on the couch to breastfeed him, something he has learned to enjoy more eagerly.

"How is that possible?" I ask and swear to myself that I need to stop sleeping with her.

"Arsim . . . ," she begins, the air between us like a dense spider's web, and I walk up to her, wrench the boy from her arms, and place him in the crib, upon which he breaks out in earsplitting wails.

"How is it possible?" I continue, and I can feel the blood rising to my head, my hands getting warmer, clenching into smoldering lumps of coal. "How can a woman who has just given birth be pregnant again? How?"

Ajshe looks at me as if sensing what is going to happen next, and I grab her by the hair and shove her across the room, hit and kick her. She sinks to the floor, clutching her stomach, wiping the edge of her mouth with her thumb, she looks up at me cheerlessly and says: "I'm sorry."

That evening I go for a walk in a park some distance from our apartment. I even stop at a restaurant for dinner, and despite the expensive bill, my mood seems to lighten. People should always get out of the house when their heart starts racing fiercely, I think, and on the way home, I buy Ajshe a bunch of flowers, which she accepts with a smile, dips her nose in among them like a teabag in water.

"Thank you," she says.

The following week Besnik and his family come to visit us; they have traveled for many hours and smell of sweat, and they have brought seven large suitcases that take up an inordinate amount of space, forcing us to watch our step as we move from one room to another.

When the children take their afternoon nap, we eat lunch and make the decision to leave tomorrow; we can't stay here a day longer.

"It's best for all of us," says Ajshe.

"That's right," I say, mimicking her tone of voice and trying to sound as though we had planned all this together, as though she hadn't done this behind my back.

Besnik holds his head in his hands and his wife stands awkwardly in the middle of the room, keeping far from the doors and windows, quivering with paranoia. She is afraid of the city, startled by the vast number of soldiers they saw on the journey. Ajshe grips her, asks her to calm down, to pull herself together for the children's sake, and explains that when you see soldiers and machine guns and tanks every day, it feels much stranger when you suddenly don't see them, and when Ajshe starts resolutely packing our belongings into suitcases, I nod in her direction, though she doesn't see it because she has her back to me, at the way she packs only the essentials, the clothes in the best condition, the photo albums, the birth and school certificates, the childcare equipment.

As evening draws in, I say I need to take care of a few things and that I'll be back early in the morning, and I run to him. I tell him about my wife, who is pregnant again, about the bus tickets to Bulgaria, our intention to move somewhere, anywhere else in Western Europe from there, and then apply for asylum, I tell him everything is paid and sorted out.

I kiss him and say I'm sorry, I'm sorry I can't stay here any longer, I would stay if I could, you believe me, don't you, I think it's for the best, best for all of us, I have a wife and I have a child and another one on the way, I have a wife, and I want to tell him how much he means to me, how I wish our shared summer could continue forever, but instead I just cry and he takes me in his arms, looks at me, his eyes fixed on me like nails, his words wading through my body. "I know, I know, I'm sorry."

When I wake up, he is gone, a five-word letter on the bed in his place, and the wardrobes are empty, the walls bare. For a while his scent hangs in the corners of the room like white ghosts, then they too process out the door, and I can't stop thinking about how pained he looked when he bade me good night, and how quietly he sobbed.

I get up and look out the window, at the thick air, heavy with
gunpowder, the people crossing the street, brittle as glass, and I
look directly at the sun, its face scratched and bleeding, its rays
beating the clouds from their course, and for a moment I think
I am about to burst into tears, but instead I smile. It is morning,
I tell myself, it's a beautiful day, it's time.

Do you remember our trip to Ulcinj? You looked so handsome at the beach and sitting opposite me at the restaurant and stepping out of the shower that for those four days my world came to a halt—do you remember that trip, the heat that sat at the dinner table with us, that tossed our salad, turning it sticky, and lingered until the next morning? How I wished the clock would stop, I wished for it so much that the sheer impossibility of it turned into an anger that raged through my life for years.

And I hated, hated everything, I hated the war, the sun and the moon, the light and the darkness, I hated the water and the air, children, I hated men, women, weapons, I hated banks, Serbs, Albanians,

Bosnians, I hated the news, the radio and television and newspapers,
I hated the streets and cars and every building—cafés, libraries,
restaurants, schools, hospitals—I hated the earth and the mountains,
hated the forest and the animals, I hated the colors of the world, hated
medicine and philosophy, books and literature, I hated the sea, hated
Europe, hated America, hated the heavens and religions, I hated Russia,
China, and India with all their pollution, Africa, I hated politics and the
police, hated god, hated the devil, hated sleep and dreams, hated waking
up in the morning, dusty unwashed windows, dirty dishes, I hated the
past, hated everything, everything you read to me, hated listening to
your pathetic stories, the smell of your breath and your curved penis,
hated the feel of it, the taste of it.

And I hated that night you said you had to go away, I hated myself
too for getting up in the early hours and packing my things and slipping
out of the apartment like an arsonist, letting you think I'd left, returned
to Kuršumlija or somewhere else, and I hated the letter you found when
you woke up, the five words I'd written down

"this is best for everyone"

did you really think that

And I hated how I walked around the city with my bags like a
homeless man, and as morning broke I went to sit at the café where
we first met, only a stone's throw from where you were right then,
and I cried in secret, hiding it from strangers, and I couldn't come
back though I almost did so, so many times—and I hated you when
I imagined you looking out of the window, realizing I was gone, that
I really was gone, I hated the way I thought of you breathing in that

empty room, hated what I imagined you doing next, packing up your belongings at my apartment, a sour burning in your throat, and closing the door behind you leaving everything we once had locked behind it, every confession, all that deranged passion, and without exception everything I'd thought was eternal was drowned out in the sound of the slamming door and the steps echoing through the stairwell that no longer belonged to either of us.

Perhaps you were relieved that I left that night, I know that you were, isn't that right, you were glad that I left you alone weren't you, sure you were, because if I hadn't been certain that you wanted me to leave, that you didn't want to embrace another morning with me, I would never have left like that, I would have stayed and suggested, how about we go back to Ulcinj or Saranda or any other town!

I would have suggested, how about you tell that woman you're not going with her, or how about you disappear without saying anything, you just never go back to her but leave with me instead—

you didn't spend a moment looking for me, you didn't look for me at all but you gave me up like an old wallet and disappeared just like that you disappeared and I was left alone in this world

that's what I hated the most

that you didn't give me the chance

to say: come with me don't go stay here

but you cried like a little brat

I expected more of you than you expected of me, maybe that was our problem all along

—

and the majesty of that hatred, oh the majesty of that hatred!

how easily it allowed me to enlist for the army, just like

that

And I SAID: I'll go to war, so be it, I'll go anywhere at all,

life passes around like a coin

ANYWHERE AT ALL, to the house of god or into the flames I'm

not afraid

of anything

The following day God slept with his daughter. As the result of their incestuous union, a deformed child was born, a blind little girl with a faint heart. "Don't say a word about this to the Devil," God told his daughter and went off to meet the Devil on a mountain pummeled by glaciers, a place where bloodhounds roamed in packs, letting out howls of hunger from their muzzles, etched with the scars of fangs, the steam of their breath rising up around the mountain in a veil of fog.

There the Devil resided, with his chimeras, inside the glacial mountain, and the subterranean tunnel that led to the Devil was full of poisonous lizards with spikes on their skin, ravens and crows that never slept but constantly flew on the spot, without permission to land, and along the walls were mummified insects, petrified clusters of gnats, crickets pressed against one another.

Once he arrived, God handed the little girl to the Devil, who grabbed her with the thumbs and forefingers of both hands, turned her upside down, and held the child closer the better to see her, to feel her feebly twitching heart against his copper chest—then they smiled at each other, the Devil with his flaming eyes and the girl with her flattened half face.

And so the Devil did as he had promised: he whistled to his snake, which, without delay, slithered its way along the fissures, forming an extension to the Devil's left arm, then with his right he gripped God's outstretched hand, and then, with the child in his arms, looked on as God departed, watched his lazy steps and slowly disappearing back.

"Fool," the Devil said to himself and shook his head in disbelief. "To hand over the daughter of God. For a single snake."

6

2003

I mourn him for years—his absence, like a dull thump across my chest. Sometimes it even feels like fear, and I'm frightened I'll somehow forget him, and I start to doubt my mind and wonder if I dreamed us up after all. Could it really be, I sometimes ask myself, that he never really existed, that he was the sky I built, a god amid a burning forest?

And then I cry, on the way to my job at the factory where I stand all day and keep watch over machines that function perfectly without me, over and over, from one day to the next. I cry in the morning as I brush my teeth. I cry as I wash my hands before dinner, as I towel myself after taking a shower, whenever I am hidden from people's eyes, because that is when he appears to me, one way or another, as memories that trample across my retina, sounds that burst through my mind, smells carrying a hint of him.

Ajshe cleans a lot, and she has become unbearably focused, that much I'll say about her. Over the years she has steadily lost weight, as though each successive child has taken its own body weight from her. As she washes the floors and windows, the laundry, the bathroom tiles, the dishes, even the walls, there's always something, she is incredibly fast in her movements, at times I don't see her at all but simply notice the result of her work. When I tell her I can't remember my mother ever washing the walls in my childhood home or dusting the surfaces every day, she explains that walls become dirty too, even if nobody touches them, even if they are bare, without a single painting, poster, or photograph.

"Have you ever been in a room when the sun shines in?" Ajshe has a habit of saying. "That's when you see how much filth people leave behind. In most weather, you can't see it."

We live in a district of high-rise apartment towers about ten kilometers from downtown in a city of millions. The neighborhood is full of identical-looking buildings, white prefabricated houses with light green, light yellow, or pink railings round their balconies. Our railings are light yellow; Ajshe thinks this is the worst possible color, of all three it's the one that gets dirty the quickest, while I think it is the best because it looks the most natural.

The building is eight stories high and we live on the second floor in an apartment with two bedrooms, a well-equipped kitchen with a breakfast bar, and a large living room with space set aside for a six-seater dining table. Still, Ajshe wishes for a larger apartment, one bedroom for our two boys and another for our beautiful, chubby daughter who was born here.

"Drita won't want to share a room with her older brothers

forever," Ajshe explains, and I remain silent because to me the apartment is big enough for the five of us—and far bigger than what we were used to in Pristina.

The building has bad sound insulation, and the Turkish family living next door is sometimes so noisy that we can't get to sleep, and Ajshe gets so annoyed at them that she's even knocked on their door and asked them to be quieter, pointing out the house rules state that after ten p.m. you can't make a racket, and when they turn their music or the television down, she sighs next to me contentedly. I don't remember her ever doing anything like that in Pristina, though the people in the apartment above us would sometimes entertain guests into the early hours.

Ajshe and her sister work part-time as stockers at a supermarket near the school our children attend. It is walking distance from our building, along the side of a busy highway with a junction leading into the parking lot of an enormous building that looks like a sports hall. Parking is free for the first two hours; if you want to stay longer, you have to pay, pop a few coins into a machine that looks like a small person who prints out a card that you're supposed to leave on the dashboard. You must move your car by the time indicated on the card. If you do not, you will get a fine.

The supermarket where Ajshe works sells absolutely everything, from exotic spices to hot tubs. In the building there is also a pharmacy, a small bookshop, a florist, customer bathrooms with baby-changing facilities—all this in two tall, open-plan floors with elevators and escalators moving tirelessly between them. Ajshe lives between our home and her workplace; that being said, she never needs to go anywhere else.

Ajshe gets annoyed at customers who, if they decide not to buy something, leave items all over the store instead of taking them back where they came from, because sometimes she has to carry them a terribly long way across the store, and it's impossible to remember where, say, the straws belong: is it with the decorations, in the drink section, or with the disposable cutlery.

"Do they think the staff have time to clear up after them? What would happen if everybody behaved like that?" Ajshe asks. "Chaos. That's what would happen. Sometimes I've deliberately ripped a product's packaging and written it off instead."

There are lots of people all around, but they don't talk much. The streets are in good shape. I've even heard that some roads have heaters beneath them to stop ice from forming, which helps to prevent traffic accidents. The roads are constantly being repaired and new ones built, new houses, shopping malls, and Ajshe and I have often wondered how so much asphalt and concrete and glass can fit in one place.

At first I thought we would only be here temporarily, that the situation in Kosovo would calm down and we would return home. I continued to believe this for a long time, but then Besnik found himself a job here and one for me too, at the same factory, and so did Ajshe and her sister, and almost without my noticing our eldest child grew and went to school, then the second, and eventually the third.

And so time passed, the years having given up on us.

Now none of them want to go back. When we meet Ajshe's sister and Besnik, we never talk of returning to Kosovo, going on instead about how lucky we were to get out, that we left Pristina at the last possible moment, that life is so much easier here, so much safer, better, that Kosovo is no place to raise children.

"What could a child become amid all that disorder?" Ajshe has been asking.

I believe that our reluctance to go back—or even to discuss the matter—is ultimately a question of money. Here there is money, in Kosovo there is none. That's more important than patriotism. Anyone who says otherwise is lying.

There are quite a lot of Kosovans here, and we meet up every now and then, organizing dinners and concerts, even starting new hobby groups; we live in our own bubble, a world within another world, like a snow globe with a house or an entire town beneath its glass dome and where glinting snowflakes start floating down when you turn it. But when you leave it alone, before long the glittering snow covers all tracks—always.

We don't spend as much time with other Albanians as maybe we should. But when you have chatted with one of them, visited one of them, you have chatted with all of them, visited all of them, because they all talk about the same things, first the corruption in Kosovo, the poverty in Kosovo, the criminality in Kosovo, the war, the war criminals still living free, then they start talking about their wages, how much they are paid for doing this and that, how much they have managed to save, enough to build a house in Kosovo, a house with two, three, four stories and mirror-glass windows on the ground floor where you can see out but not in, says one of them, while another says that his house has three bathrooms and a third says he has built a garage on the side of his house, heated all year round and big enough to swallow up three vehicles.

Ajshe often wonders why they are building such big houses in Kosovo in the first place, spending such vast sums of money on empty properties.

"Because they're not planning on moving back, are they?" she asks.

I agree with her. It's just for show; it makes absolutely no sense to live in cramped conditions for eleven months of the year just to spread yourself out for a few weeks.

Each spring, Ajshe and I talk about visiting Kosovo, but summer always arrives before we get around to buying tickets, and we end up staying put—all because of the short, fragmented vacations we get from work, or so we tell ourselves.

Just like Ajshe, my children are afraid of me these days. To my sons, Driton and Endrit, and my daughter, Drita, I am a distant, strange man. To be honest, I don't know exactly why I smack them, from lack of anything better to do or because I think they really deserve punishment for bad behavior at school, for impudence and misbehaving at the dinner table.

Or is it because I think that it's better to be afraid of something than not to be afraid of anything, is it because that's how I grew up, just like every Albanian I know: smacked around by my parents, and generally with good reason, I think to this day. You should fear your father's hands and run to your mother's arms, and when there is no longer a father to fear or a mother to run to, then you live in fear of illness and pain, fear of rashes and infections, microbes, bacteria, fear of falling asleep, you fear authority, traffic, a lamp falling from the ceiling during the night, you fear everything, everything, just like you feared your father.

One raised with fear never learns to live without it. When you take away its cause, fear manifests, becoming its own consequences—a lingering suspicion, hallucinations and waking dreams. And when a fearful person loses the ability to let go of their fear, fear is then transfigured: it is the neighbor with a better parking space because this is his country, not yours; it is a dog walker nodding in your direction as you pass each other and squinting, not to say hello but because you are a foreigner; a checkout assistant sighing while scanning the marked-down sandwiches you have bought for the freezer, not out of boredom but because you are an intruder behaving unfairly toward others;

a manager shaking his head, not out of frustration but because you don't understand instructions in their language.

Drita is a kind and well-behaved girl, but our sons get into fights at school almost every day. Their teachers tell me and Ajshe that our sons' problems are all because we moved here from Kosovo. It's a difficult situation for a young child, they explain. Living between two languages, two cultures and religions can cause an identity crisis, and the children no longer know who they are, because their entire world is formed from such conflicting customs and practices, they tell us flatly, as though informing us of an upcoming renovation.

It irritates and riles us, because their words imply that our children's lives are somehow incomplete or lacking in some crucial respect, that because of us their lives aren't healthy and full, because we moved here to escape the war. To their minds, the fact that our children speak several languages fluently, that they are acquainted with different customs and beliefs apparently doesn't enrich our sons' lives; on the contrary, they see it as a strain. Their teachers think that our children don't need Albanian as much as the languages spoken and taught at school, that there isn't anything left behind in Kosovo without which they won't get along or about which they should learn more than the subjects they teach. On occasion I've flicked through their schoolbooks and noticed there isn't any mention of Kosovo, not a single word about Yugoslavia, of the grand, glittering life of affluence that people once enjoyed there.

Ajshe tries to tell them that our children are perfect and whole just the way they are, they are beautiful and innocent, that the boys only get into trouble because they are constantly being reminded of the war, of the fact that they are Kosovans, though nowadays they speak another language far better than they will ever speak Albanian.

"This only segregates them from their classmates," Ajshe tells them.

When our children don't do well in exams, instead of giving them extra support the teachers simply shrug their shoulders, saying the children's lack of success is down to being bilingual. When our children start a fight at school, instead of telling them that hitting other kids is wrong, they say that although you came here in the middle of a violent conflict, here we don't put up with violence, here we don't hit other people, and when they are late for school or disturb other students in class, instead of giving them a detention, the teachers just say this isn't Kosovo, you know, in this country we turn up on time and respect other students' right to learn in peace.

"Would the teachers say the boys aren't getting on at school just because they're bilingual if their mother tongue was something else?" Ajshe continues. "Even little children can accomplish great things, but if you constantly remind them they are not the equal of everyone else, that they don't deserve something they want or that they're no good at anything, before long they start to believe it, they think it must be true because everybody says so: they don't deserve anything, they can't do anything properly, they're no good at anything. Then, sure, they won't do as well as they might otherwise."

Ajshe won't let the matter drop, but almost every month she goes to the school to talk with the teachers and the other parents. Even using a professional interpreter, she's tried to explain to them that we consider the school to be racist and that children don't think about where they come from, adults barely think about it either, she's tried to tell them that our children should be punished when they misbehave and that teachers should expect the same standards of them as they do of all the other children, not a fraction less, and that they must not be shown lenience simply because their parents are refugees. It's not a reason and it's certainly not an excuse, she has tried to explain.

In the evenings, Ajshe is often worried that she hasn't been able to express herself clearly, that the teachers have spoken over her, shaken their heads, patronized her, saying, do you realize that in this country you need a university degree if you want to become a schoolteacher, and it takes years of dedication to get one.

"How is it in Kosovo? Have you gone to university?" they ask her, and Ajshe is left unable to answer but starts cursing them on her way home and continues ranting to me later on.

"I don't know," she often sighs in bed before going to sleep. "They could make so much more of themselves here," she says. "Couldn't they?" she adds, though she knows I won't have anything to say.

Then she switches off the lights.

"Sleep well."

The nights are easier. When Ajshe is sleeping heavily beside me and the children are in their own room, nobody asks me for anything, nobody asks me what time I'll be home, whether I'll have time to stop on the way to pick up some milk, whether I can give them money for the mall, a school outing, or whether I could buy toys and instruments that the children ask for in a way that doesn't feel like a request so much as a necessity. And all I can do is agree, though the devices I buy them are ludicrously expensive and cost more than several months' wages in Kosovo. In other respects we try to save any money left over and to live as frugally as possible, we buy cheap and secondhand things instead of new.

At times I fret about everything long into the night; the worry about whether we'll have enough money, about what kind of people our children will grow up to be makes me cough so much that I have to sit up in bed. I go out to the balcony for a cigarette, then I sit down at the computer, surf the internet and read the news until I start to feel tired. Every time I type Miloš's name into the search engine, I feel nervous, but month after month the results that come up take me to the same sites, telling me about people with the same name but never about him, and I scroll through the same pages I've read dozens of times before, all the while peering over my shoulder.

Every morning I get out of bed tired, awake to another stagnant, identical day, whereas Ajshe appears to sleep perfectly well and without any interruption; she is always busy doing something, looking after our home, our children, moving the fridge to clean behind it, even vacuuming the cupboards as if simply to kill time.

Ajshe can see I'm not myself here; it's not a secret that I want to leave, for good. And I can see from her that she doesn't dare bring up the subject because she is afraid that if I decide that we are leaving, she will have no option but to obey me. Instead, she says things like: *What a beautiful day it is today.* Or: *Spring is on its way, the flowers will soon be in bloom, though it's still cold and rainy, I'm going to make your favorite food this weekend and you can sleep as long as you need, sleep off all that fatigue, you can read and write in peace if you want, I can take the children somewhere in the meantime, to the park or into town.*

Some days are tolerable and things at home are peaceful. Ajshe knows not to talk to me for a while after I've slapped one of our screaming, misbehaving children, calling them spoiled, wretched, useless, ungrateful brats who will never be good for anything, never turn into decent people.

"If you were in Kosovo, you'd have nothing, you'd be walking around scared shitless and begging for food in the street," I often shout at them, and they hide under their beds and cry or leave the apartment vowing never to come back, to report me to the police, saying I'll go to jail where I belong because I am a *dreq,* a devil.

But after a while they always come home again, and Ajshe tells them their father didn't mean to be cruel, though on some level I did mean every word I said. They are spoiled from all this luxury, from having life too easy.

Sometimes, while putting her favorite flowers in a vase and displaying them on the table or the windowsill, or after washing the linoleum floors in our apartment by hand, I have seen a flash of contentment in Ajshe's expression, I can almost hear her thinking, *This is good, everything is fine, everything will work out.*

Then she smiles at the flowers or her gleaming, flawless work for a moment before hurrying on to the next chore. At times like this I too am content, I feel more than mere inadequacy, I am more upbeat, I am needed—not a burden on Ajshe, who would doubtless survive here without me, not a nuisance to my children, who never turn to me for help because they know I don't understand, and probably never will understand to the same extent the language that they speak so effortlessly with one another.

Despite their young age, the children know this much about their father: my father isn't the same as other fathers because my father can't do the things other fathers do, and I don't really need him for anything. And knowing this bothers me surprisingly little.

Then there are other days when I think horrific thoughts— and at those moments I have to pull over to the side of the road or go to the park, sit down and take deep breaths, because I've come so, so close to doing a U-turn and crashing into the side of a truck, throwing myself off the railings at the mall, or jumping in front of a bus or metro, and once I've calmed down and realize that what stopped me wasn't the knowledge that I'd be leaving behind a wife and children but the fear that I might actually survive, my heart starts to turn.

The war ended long ago, but the end of it doesn't really mean anything. Ajshe says that the real war starts with the cessation of hostilities and the signing of a peace treaty, because this is when you can see the earliest consequences of war, the havoc into which war has driven a country.

It's aptly put, because we Albanians are washed across the world like a handful of sand scattered into the sea, we have disappeared into the landscape like a wooden altar screen against a wooden altar. Our country is forever tainted, it has been violated with malicious words, demarcated in the maps of the world with a dashed black line.

It's easy to despise this life and everything about it because none of it is mine.

is it wrong to get an erection while your father rapes you

is it wrong to get an erection while your brother rapes you

is it wrong to push a killer off the roof, to throw a sick cat into

boiling water

can you have an abortion if the child is disabled can you commit

suicide if you have a wife and children can you even if you don't

can you steal from the poor if you are poorer still

is it wrong to want to be alone with your father or brother though

you know they will rape you

is it wrong to wish for it at night—to wish for your father or brother to

rape you

or both of them

again

and again

what if your father rapes your sister

what if you feel envious that your father rapes your sister instead of you

can you kill your sister then

out of envy

can you steal food if you are hungry

and clothes if you are cold

what about medicine for the sick

can you walk right into the pharmacy with a gun then

my sister took her own life

she was thirteen

she hanged herself from a tree at night I found her in the morning

I was on my way to let the cows out of the barn

and my sister was dangling from a branch like a salmon on a hook,

in her white nightgown

my father had raped her

my brother had raped her

I screamed for my life though my sister looked unharmed, unconquered

I'll never forget that sight

my father, my mother, my brother came running, they were crying can you feel envy toward the dead I wondered and looked at my

sister's groin

the grass beneath her feet it was black

I got an erection when my father slept with me the next day

he called me by my sister's name, that slut

I'll kill my father, I swore to myself, next time

I'll kill my father

it is right it is perfect, I said

my father raped me many times after that

and it felt good, I didn't want it to stop

it was so wrong it was sick I suppose

I am repulsive, later on I said

sorry

to the heavens

One morning I woke up early, before daybreak, like a cat. I packed a

pair of pants and a few shirts in a plastic bag, a bar of soap, a notepad

and a pen, my father's savings from behind the upper cupboard in the

kitchen

then I gathered a large pile of old newspapers on the couch in the living

room and another beneath the kitchen table and a third in front of the

wardrobe in the hallway and I poured gasoline over them and over the

carpets and the curtains and the furniture, everything was as calm as a slow waltz in a beautiful dream, and I let the animals out of their cages and stables and then I set everything ablaze, the whole ground floor one room at a time, and my footsteps were like velvet, droplets of water in the ocean currents, and my father and my brother and my mother were asleep upstairs and I glided away from the house, as if I was flying, and above the roar of the fire I heard my father shouting something and my mother screaming and then the gas cylinders in the kitchen exploded, severing the sounds surging from the house's openings, and the animals broke into a ferocious stampede, they were carefree now, and eventually without looking behind me I walked to the top of a nearby hill and sat down and said to myself good, good, good; I am good, I'm good, I am good, then I continued on my way to the station where I got on the next bus, it took me to Belgrade, the white city, straight to my new life, and after sitting down in my seat I wrote those words, vertically and horizontally, so that I would never forget, so that I would always remember—I am good I am good I am free

On the way I imagined them burning alive. At first it didn't feel like anything at all, and then it felt good.

I wrote terrible things the other day; I'm still trembling though I've been doing lots of strength and stretching exercises. Those things didn't really happen, but I imagined them, and more besides, they would have all deserved it. Maybe I was just ashamed to admit that I left the way I did, pathetically, secretly, in the middle of the night while the rest of the house was asleep on their dirty sheets . . .

but it's just as true all the same, they are just as dead to me still

I should apologize to you I've lied and keep lying

about so many things

sometimes it's as if the evil you see becomes the evil you do

7

2003

After writing to each other online for a couple of weeks, he suggests we meet for the first time in real life. We have been messaging in a chat room almost every evening for a few weeks, talking about our favorite foods, our favorite books, movies, music, TV shows, school, hobbies, and I can't remember the last time I felt this energetic coming back from work than during this time.

He sent me a smiley face, that's how it all started when he saw my pictures on my profile—standard images of men's torsos that I'd found online but that might as well have been pictures of my own body. Unlike mine, his profile features a real photograph of himself, so young and so beautiful, I think the first time I see his picture, which he has taken lying in bed, perhaps after waking up on a lazy weekend morning. In the photograph he has a pillow on his chest, almost hiding behind it, and he is smiling coyly at the camera.

I became increasingly attracted to him, and the feeling grew all the more as he told me about himself, how well he'd done on his exams, the strategy and role-playing games that occupy him late into the night, about the walls of his room, which he has plastered with posters of pop and rock bands, about his mother, who works as an architect, and his elder brother, who studies information technology at the university. His father lives at another address, *and it's just as well,* he says, *I hate him.* There's something alluring about him, something almost delectable, innocent, trusting, and sensitive.

"Can you send me a face pic?" he asks the day before we meet.

"You know I can't," I reply. "I can't take the risk—I'm married and have children. But people have told me I'm quite handsome, and I'm a nice, down-to-earth guy with a sense of humor. Trust me."

"I'm nervous," he writes.

"I know, me too," I reply. "Me too."

"What if you don't like me face-to-face?" The question pops up on the screen, and when I don't respond immediately he sends another message, this one with only three dots.

"Don't be silly. You're a fine young man," I write. "Really pretty. I'm sure I'll like you."

"I'm actually really ugly," he writes. "You'll run a mile when you see me. I bet you will."

"No, no," I reply. "You're funny. So, see you tomorrow?"

The following day he arrives at the gas station we agreed upon, ahead of time, just like me. He has cycled five kilometers, far enough away from his house and people he might bump into, and all he knows is the make and color of my car—a dark gray Opel—

and that I'll be standing next to it in the parking lot wearing a pair of sunglasses.

I see him at a distance, the woeful way he pedals his bike, without a helmet, his sturdy, bone-white fingers gripping the handlebars, and when he sees me, he wipes the sweat from his brow with a nonchalant flick of his right hand, rides in front of the gas-station door, locks his bike to the stand, and begins walking toward me, confidently, his expression set, his chest chubby.

He is wearing a pair of worn-out denim shorts, his pale legs, covered in bruises, jutting from beneath them, as though unconnected to the rest of his body, and a brown long-sleeved T-shirt, which he is constantly pulling down, and on his feet a pair of red sneakers that look dirty and too small for him.

The closer he comes, the more pained my smile, the heavier the weight that has appeared above my stomach. He is much chunkier than in the photographs he sent me; his chest sags and his hips are like those of a grown woman, and his bangs hang down across his cheeks, as if to hide his pocked skin. He told me he regularly works out, goes running and swimming, but it doesn't look like it; instead he looks slightly ill, a rather sickly version of a middle-aged man, though he is seventeen.

I begin to regret ever agreeing to meet him.

"How's it going?" I ask once he's standing in front of me. I remove my sunglasses and try not to let my disappointment show. "Shall we go?" I suggest as he mumbles something in reply, and beneath the roar of a passing motorbike all I can make out is that he isn't asking me the same question.

"Yes," he says, flicks his bangs again, and walks to the other side of the car as though we are in a hurry, opens the door, and hops into the passenger seat.

———

We head for McDonald's, about ten kilometers away, just as we've agreed. I decide that once we're done, I'll take him back to the gas station, he will fetch his bike and cycle home, and I will no longer respond to his messages, and we will never see each other again.

"So, what do you think of me?" he asks all of a sudden, looking at me out of the corner of his eye.

His slightly raised shoulder only emphasizes his bad posture, and he has crossed his arms over his belly. I don't reply but keep driving along the blurred road narrowing ahead.

"I knew it," he says after a pause and demonstratively turns his head away. "You don't want me," he adds, staring out of the window at the landscape opening up in vivid autumnal splendor, the brazen evening sunshine, and the trees, their branches resplendent, almost boastful.

"No, no," I say. "You look good, really good." The words just come out of my mouth; I take off my sunglasses and then, though I can hear my mind resisting, I place my right hand on his left thigh and squeeze a little. "You are beautiful," I add instinctively and smile.

"Really?" he says, his voice childish; his eyes turn first to my hand then my eyes, and again he swipes at his bangs.

"Yes."

Just as I am about to take my hand away, he places his own upon it; tacky with sweat, his warm, pudgy fingers spread across the back of my hand like leeches.

"You're really handsome," he simpers. "Like, really handsome, much handsomer than I was expecting," he repeats, then adds a "wow," and my body is unable to obey my brain, which implores me to turn back, to stop touching him.

———

We arrive at the packed, noisy restaurant and stand in line at the counter; he wants a Big Mac meal with supersize fries, a drink, and a large chocolate milkshake. I only order a coffee for myself, because for some reason his order embarrasses me.

It feels as though the entire restaurant knows we are on a date, though I realize that to outsiders we might look like brothers. Once we have our food and drinks, we sit down at a two-seater table. He goes straight for the fries, dipping one end in ketchup and the other in mayonnaise.

"Why aren't you eating anything?" he asks with his mouth full, and as I try to pick up one of the fries I've paid for, he bats my hand away.

"Get your own!" he snaps.

"I'm not really hungry," I tell him and try, unsuccessfully, to muster a smile. "You eat."

He greedily unwraps the burger and slurps his sugar-free soda and milkshake one after the other, his eyes wide, stuffs the fries into his mouth four, five at a time, and takes absurdly large bites out of his burger, which he seems to swallow almost without chewing.

"You realize that food is quite unhealthy?" I ask him across the table.

He stops eating and looks up at me, his expression pained.

"What do you mean?"

"I mean you shouldn't eat this kind of food very often," I reply in a fatherly tone. "It'll make you fat," I add bluntly, knowing full well that he must have learned this at school.

He drops half of the burger onto the tray and pushes it away, stands up, wipes his hands on his shorts, and walks to the bathroom without saying a word.

He spends such a long time in there that I even consider slipping away, maybe he wishes I would disappear too, I wonder, but he's so far away from his bike and even farther from home that it simply wouldn't be right to run off and abandon him, I reason with myself. As I sit there waiting for him, I think how stupid this is and how stupid I am, how I don't know anything about him though I thought I knew a lot, and I feel angry at his lies. What did he think they would achieve? He should already know that lying is never the answer, that the truth will always out.

He returns to the table, his eyes bloodshot.

"Take me back," he says and blows his nose.

"Good," I say, and he walks out of the restaurant.

As I return the tray to the collection point, I feel a great sense of relief. We set off in a mood of awkward silence. When we are halfway there, he starts nervously fidgeting in his seat, staring in turn out of the window and at me. I don't look over at him but concentrate on driving us back to the familiar gas station, but when he puts a hand on my thigh, which at first I move away but which he instantly returns, this time to my groin, and when he starts caressing my testicles and asks if he can suck me off in the car, I drive past the familiar gas station and turn at the next junction onto a smaller road, from the smaller road onto a narrow dirt track leading to the edge of a disused sports field.

I don't know where we are, and I switch off the engine but leave the radio on. After this, his fingers trembling, the boy undoes my belt and I raise my pelvis as he pulls down my pants.

"You're really handsome," he says nervously and pulls my underpants farther down. "Really handsome."

I briefly catch his eye, and he looks so sad that I grab him round the back of the head and push his face into my groin. He barely knows what to do, his teeth are constantly scratching delicate areas, and he only takes the glans into his mouth, sucking it like he did his milkshake, without using his tongue and paying no attention to the shaft, which he treats more like a door handle.

In giving me oral sex, he sounds like a moose injured in a car accident. I ejaculate in his mouth quickly, without warning, and when I hear him swallowing, I guide his head away and fasten my pants.

"Thank you," he says as I start the engine.

He wipes his mouth on his wrist, the car smells of chlorine, sweaty armpits, moist groin, flesh, and grease. Suddenly I find him amusing; he is revolting, I think, he eats at McDonald's every day, eats everything he can get his hands on, at home he runs between his messy bedroom and the refrigerator and eats, eats, eats, and eats, stuffs himself full of fat and sugar, licks the plates, the pots and pans clean and slurps up every last drop of his soda, then burps. I can imagine him smuggling packets of cookies, ice-cream cones, bags of chips, boxes of chocolates under his clothes, munching on candy in the dark and hiding the wrappers at the bottom of the trash can.

Without delay, I drive back to the highway, and then he starts sniveling.

"What now?" I ask through a forced smile.

His whimpering erupts into a torrent of sobs, the air bursts out of him in a series of sharp splutters, and he buries his face in his hands, wipes his snotty hands on his shorts, letting the spittle run down his chin and dribble onto his chest.

"You think I'm ugly," he stammers. "Don't you?" he continues and looks up at me through weepy eyes.

I stare at the road ahead and put my foot on the gas, I want to get back as quickly as possible, to get rid of this unstable, hysterical person, while at the same time swearing to myself I'll never again meet up with anyone under twenty.

"Everything's fine," I tell him.

Finally the familiar ramp comes into view, and behind that the tower of the gas station rises like a chimney from a house. As I pull up near his bike, he mercifully calms down a little, perhaps there's a level of comfort in seeing his property again; he will be able to cycle home, where life will continue just as it had before he met me, and one day he will be able to erase this sorry episode from his mind altogether.

But he doesn't move to open the door and again asks me if I think he is ugly. I do think he's ugly, and I feel like asking him why he sent misleading pictures of himself and assured me he was different from how he is in real life, and as he presses me for an answer a third time I become so enraged that I reach across, open his door, and start pushing him out of the car.

"Go home," I shout, and he is so startled by my outburst that he clambers out of the car, shuts the door, and scuttles off toward his bike.

And there he remains. As I pull away, I glance in his direction and see his hunched back, his arms wrapped round his stomach, his tearstained cheeks drooping beneath his closed eyes.

In the days that follow he sends me dozens of text messages:

I'm sorry I lied to you.
I knew I wouldn't be good enough as myself.
That's why I sent those pictures.
I'm sorry you don't think I'm attractive.
I can't help it.
I'm sorry I'm so fat.
I was wearing bad clothes.
I've got nicer ones.
Much nicer ones.
I'll do whatever you want.
Please answer.
I'm sorry. Can you just answer?
You're so handsome.

I promise I'll lose weight.
Can I see you?
I want you to be my boyfriend.
Can you say something?
Are you even getting these messages?
We can do what we did in the car again, every day.
If you want.
No pressure.
Every day, loads of times.
As often as you want.
OK?
OK?
Can we meet today?
Or tomorrow?
As often as you want.
Many times a day.
I liked it.
You don't have to do anything in return.
Because I love you.
Do you get it?
I love you.
Answer me!
Can you just answer me?

A week later the police turn up at my workplace. At first they are shown to my supervisor, who then leads them to my workstation. As I see them approaching, it feels as though the entire factory falls silent, the cutting machines turn cold, and my colleagues move more stiffly, as if making space for what happens next.

Upon seeing the police, the natural instinct for someone like me is to run away, but if you can't do that, the mind starts fleeing instead, traversing moments chiseled with despair and remorse, unrepented deeds and sins that corrode the mind, and at times those moments are so broken and full of misery, so far in the past, that the mind forgets to return, and I find myself unable to hear what it is the officers are asking me.

This is the most humiliating thing that has ever happened to me, is the first thought once my mind is finally able to form them again, but as the police lead me out of the building, across the factory floor, and through countless doors and corridors, the shame quickly fades: this life, I tell myself and close my eyes as if I no longer needed them, this life ends now.

Belgrade is a beautiful city, drenched in disinfectant.

When I arrived I had so much money, and because I had so much money I thought I owned everything, the restaurants, the cafés, and shops because I could eat and drink and buy whatever I wanted, and there was so much money that paper money seemed to multiply into more paper money and coins, so that eventually I didn't need to count it anymore.

Until there came a point when I didn't have any money, suddenly I was homeless, I was about to freeze, to be robbed of what little I still had.

How stupid we can be when we have plenty, how blind we are to

luxury. I don't know of anything more aggravating than the belly
flop that follows when you realize you're prepared to do anything, say
anything at all to retrieve just a fraction of what was once so abundant.

It was then that I had to start talking to god, though I'd never
believed in him: god give me a reason to be here AND help me I beg
you AND I know I've never spoken your name in the way I'm speaking
it now

surely that means something too—
and god knew what I left unsaid: that if he didn't hear me at my
most desperate he would never hear from me again

isn't it bizarre that even people of no faith still invoke god
in a moment of need—
And so god gave me a reason: god gave me him. God brought him
to me, sat him down on a Belgrade park bench on the greenest day of
summer, and made him say hello to me as I walked past. You there,
god's creation called out, and I turned only to be impressed by his
heroic body, alongside which my own body looked like a trampled leaf
next to a majestic oak tree, and he had rugged, chiseled arms too, his
face pointed forward like the hood of a truck.

sit down—that's what he said to me,
sit down

I walked right up to him, because that's what you do when a man
like that beckons you over, and once I was close I first wanted to
immortalize him, to scratch him into a tree, his wide nose and large,
drooping ears, his sharp chin and bulging eyes, his thick, silken black
hair like the bristles of a brush, his shovel hands and canoe feet in black,

stretched leather shoes, and quivering I asked him, who are you, did god send you, did you come here at god's command, and the man remained silent and gave me an enigmatic smile, and when I finally sat down next to him, adrift from myself, my eyes swollen, I asked him again: is it you, can it really be you, so you finally decided to come—

and the man simply smiled, placed a forefinger beneath my chin, and said

"hey, kiddo"

8

2003

I am interrogated several times. Different officers ask me the same questions, and I do my best to always respond in the same way. Yes, we wrote to each other online and we decided to meet in person, we had a bite to eat at a hamburger restaurant and after that we drove somewhere discreet and he gave me oral sex in the car, yes, I admit that's what happened but I didn't force him to do anything, it can't be a crime if he wanted it to happen, he suggested it to me himself as I was driving him back to the gas station where he'd left his bike.

I deny guilt for what I am accused of, and at every opportunity I try to remind the authorities that the boy told me he was seventeen, not fourteen, that he looked much older, but none of this matters, they tell me I should have known, asked to see his ID. He is just a child and cannot be held responsible for his actions, they say, juveniles have no idea what they are doing, and from their reactions to my attempts to defend myself I learn not to argue with them, as I can feel I'm only making the situation worse by telling them that he sent me text messages after our meeting too, messages in which he said he loved me, wanted me to be his boyfriend.

I am assigned a lawyer, who seems reluctant to represent me. He is a man younger than me, in his late twenties and still inexperienced, I guess, because he looks at me in a way that is reserved only for certain kinds of people. People like me. People for whom it isn't appropriate to feel anything. He has a transcript of the full correspondence between me and the boy, the situation isn't looking good, I know that, and from our conversations I expect there is no doubt that I will be found guilty and that my lawyer will try to negotiate the most lenient sentence on my behalf, it might even be mitigated by the fact that I'm a first-time offender, and apparently my case would be viewed more favorably if I admitted guilt and showed remorse.

Throughout the weeks of investigation, I am angry and absentminded, I cannot control myself and can't express my thoughts clearly, I refuse the interpreter they offer me, as though someone else has taken my place and I am merely following this other person's actions from the side. I lash out at my children and pull their hair for the smallest reasons, I hit Ajshe too because she infuriates me by constantly asking what I'm doing, about the upcoming weekend, the next week, and the following month, always double-checking our schedules, talking, talking incessantly. I park my car wherever I want, I don't care, and in the evenings I often drive out to the same gas station where we first met, in the hope that I might see the boy again so that I could knock his teeth down his throat, punch his nose until it is broken and deformed, run him over, and drive away.

Sometimes I give in to my temptations and sign in to the chat room again, though I know I mustn't and shouldn't, that the authorities can trace every click of my computer. After scrolling through the list of nicknames online and noting that there's no sign of the boy, I start chatting with the other users in disappointment. Some of them want to meet up and have sex in a car or somewhere in the forest, a cheap hotel, others just send me suggestive messages, and others ask me to exchange photographs and masturbate with them on the webcam, and sometimes I agree.

In the weeks before the trial, I keep coming back to a thought I first heard from my father a long time ago. He once said it's good to experience misery and distress, because only misery and distress can prepare you for the day when misery and distress return, because it always happens, he said; they always come back.

"The world is rotten," I say to Ajshe one morning.

"Yes, Arsim, it is," she replies, lifts a box of eggs and a frying pan onto the kitchen counter, and sits down opposite me.

"I stole a doll from a store last week," she says slowly, a hint of fear in her voice. "Drita was crying for one as though she was deranged and lay down on the floor in the middle of the toy department!" Ajshe exclaims. "You should have seen her, goodness it was embarrassing, she refused to let go of that damned doll. So I stole it, I stuffed it beneath a pile of clothes and went into the changing room pretending to try on some dresses and sweaters, and there I opened the packet, slipped the doll into my bag, left the rubbish beneath the pile of clothes in the booth, and walked out."

Then Ajshe begins to cry.

"I'm sorry," she says, blowing her nose into a scrap of tissue. "But it was terribly expensive. And she played with the doll for a few hours, then forgot all about it," Ajshe continues, shaking her head and apologizing again. "I've been really nervous and on edge recently. Why might that be?" she asks.

I look helplessly in her eyes, which alternate between guilt, shame, and anger.

"What do you think? Should we move back to Kosovo?" she asks after a moment's silence. "The children are still small," she argues, and I am certain she has heard about my arrest from her sister.

"I really don't know," she continues the conversation with herself. "Did you hear they've started paying people to go back to their homeland? It's not much apparently, but you'll get by for a little while, possibly even long enough to get your life in order. We could rent a big apartment in Pristina, I could look for work there too. Besides, at this time of year the price of watermelon is ridiculously low, here they're not nearly as sweet . . ."

I interrupt her and tell her I met up with a young woman I came across on the internet and that now I'm being accused of a crime, the sexual abuse of a minor. I tell her the girl said she was seventeen, I didn't know she was fourteen, it's a serious crime here, then I tell her about the gas station, the authorities, the interrogations and all the details, the upcoming trial, all this flows from my mouth like a shopping list, like an account of what I got up to that day, and when I finish Ajshe looks out of the window at the three apartment buildings opposite, identical copies of our own, the strip of brightening sky where the clouds have gathered in military formation, and the few trees standing in the yard like soldiers.

"What? Is it money the damn girl's after?" Ajshe asks angrily. "Surely she knows we haven't got much money?"

"I don't know," I reply.

"Then we can't leave yet." She sighs calmly, without looking at me, folds the tissue in her fist, calmly stands up, throws it in the garbage, and turns on the stove and slides the pan across the burner, breaking the silence that gradually fills with the growing crackle of eggs frying in the slowly warming pan.

The trial takes place in a court that resembles a school classroom, and there are only a fistful of people present as the case is heard behind closed doors. The judge sits in front of us, a pile of paperwork on his desk, behind him are a few framed photographs of lakeside scenery, and us, the accusers and the accused, both with their legal representatives; we are sitting in front of him on long benches as though we were in church. I'm not sure why I'm surprised to notice that, instead of the boy himself, it's his parents who have come to the courtroom, looking angry and humiliated. I guess I had hoped to see the boy again, hoped that my seeing him or his seeing me would help bring all this madness to an end.

A woman wearing glasses and a black pantsuit is sitting with her arms folded, and beside her sits a man in a dark gray sweater and black jeans, blushing, almost as though he were trying to hide behind the woman. They don't look like the boy's parents at all, they don't even look like parents, let alone a former married couple, but as though they have suddenly awoken to find they have a shared child. They don't so much as glance at me throughout the hearing, though I constantly try to make eye contact with them.

The atmosphere is so tense that everything hurtles past me; it all happens as if by itself. I am strangely indifferent to the pro-

ceedings and almost can't fully understand what the judge is saying, the heated summation by the prosecutor or my own lawyer's
defense plea, and it feels as though I am following a concert or
the life of a complete stranger from inside my car; again I become
inconspicuous, a framed photograph on the wall of a room filled
with legal jargon.

The prosecutor, a relatively manly woman in her fifties who
speaks in a strong, resonant voice, froths for a while, then the
judge says something, and my lawyer gesticulates and grimaces
as if he is ashamed and doesn't want to be here, steadies himself against the edge of the table and nervously fidgets with the
papers on the desk, he seems stupid and helpless and woefully
underprepared for my case, then the judge says something else
and soon it's all over, the charges are read, the guilty party is sentenced, and justice is served.

How can they do this, I wonder, how can they compress so
many people's fates into a handful of convoluted sentences?

I burst out laughing. I can't help it. I don't know where it
comes from, but that's what happens. Everybody, the judge, the
boy's parents, the prosecutor, and my lawyer look at me with
unbridled disdain, in the same way that I imagine I would look
at them in a similar situation, and I do everything I can to try to
suppress my emotions, but it just makes things worse so I allow
the gale of laughter to erupt freely.

For some reason I think of ridiculous, irrelevant things, like
the boy, now a victim of gross sexual abuse, tripping over his
shoelaces and starting to cry about the ice cream now flattened
beneath his stomach, then I imagine my daughter and how one
day when we were in the park she called an old man walking past
an idiot, it came out of nowhere, and how delicious a situation it
was because she had never used that word before, and I think of
my younger son, whom I once placed on the mechanical horse in

the shopping mall, and I looked at his smile, at the boundless joy that shone from his eyes as he looked back at me, a man he didn't even know, a man to whom his happiness should mean everything, and it pained me how little that boy knew about his father.

I have brought three children into this world, each of whom I have probably tainted forever, I think, and the thought snaps my laughter's neck asunder.

I made them, I brought them here.

I am going to prison, it hits me, you have been sentenced to thirteen months' incarceration, they repeat this to me, and the court finds my crime and "case"—this is the word they use—so serious that once I have served my sentence I will be deported from the country, I hear them decree.

"Good." The word escapes my mouth accompanied by a strange sneer, and when they inform me that I can appeal the decision in the higher court, I tell them I don't want to, that I accept the ruling.

Only once I have relinquished my personal effects am I allowed to phone Ajshe, and when I have told her I am in police custody, about to go to prison, that I won't be coming home for some while, at least thirteen months, that I can't understand how this happened, I hear her swear—for the first time ever.

"*Dreqi të hangt,*" she says. "May the Devil eat you," she repeats in a voice that is as sad as it is furious.

"I'm sorry," I reply. "I don't know what to say."

She is breathing so heavily, so deeply, that I think she must be gathering the strength to say she never wants to see me again, that she wants to continue her life with the children, to move on without me, that this is the last time we will ever speak.

"I'll tell the children you've gone on holiday," she informs me after a short pause. "No. I'll tell them you've gone to Kosovo to build us a house, Arsim, they are still small, don't worry about it, they won't remember this when they grow up, at their age thirteen months is nothing, you know how children's minds work, time is different for them than for us. It passes painfully slowly, but a moment later they can't remember a single thing about it."

"Ajshe," I say sluggishly.

"Quiet!" she shouts in a voice that no longer sounds like her own. "I'll focus their attention on other things while you're gone, I'll ask for extra shifts, we'll be fine, send me the address of the prison and I'll come and visit, it's only thirteen months, Arsim. Thirteen months."

"I don't want you to visit, Ajshe."

"Why not? I've heard the conditions in prisons here are very comfortable, you can even study or write, if you want."

"Yes."

"You'd like that. You can think of it as a sort of holiday. That's what you've been waiting for, right?"

"That's not the reason."

"Then what is it? My sister? Besnik? They'll understand. Or are you thinking about other people? Don't worry about other people, I'll tell them all the same story, nobody will know where you are, and if someone does find out, then I'll turn my back on them before they get a chance to do so to me, I'll tell them, get out of my sight, you are nothing to my family."

"I don't want . . . you, this, anymore. I don't love you, Ajshe. Don't you see?" I whisper, and once I've said it out loud I feel an enormous sense of relief, like lying down in a cool bed after an exhausting day.

For a moment she is quiet at the other end of the phone, and during that silence I imagine the words I have spoken sinking to the bottom of her stomach, wandering along her veins, and settling in her heart and mind. She must have been expecting to hear this for a long time, and now that I've said it, placed the words between us, they can never be taken back again.

"Of course you love me," she replies curtly. "Because if you didn't love me and the children in some way, you wouldn't be calling me now. Isn't that right?"

"Yes," I say. "I suppose so."

"Because sometimes love means being with someone, anyone, just so you're not alone. Nobody deserves the cruelty of loneliness. So I will wait for you, Arsim. Please know that you will be in my thoughts every single second. Call me when you can. Give me the address where I can write to you, visit you, whatever you want."

This woman never gives up, I think, and I can only hold back the sense of revulsion I feel as she asks: "Is that clear?"

After the call I am led into a police cell to await the following morning, when I will be transported to prison. The cell is gray and windowless, a room battered with bright yellow light, its brick walls full of scrawls of which I don't understand much. It is the lowliest place I have ever been. In one corner of the room is a small metal sink and toilet bowl, and in the other a thin foam mattress the same color as the light; it is full of holes and smells of old urine. I sit down on it, my knees pulled against my mouth, I feel so horribly cold.

The first hours are the worst. I crack, shout, cry, hit and kick the walls, the sink, the toilet, the mattress, and myself, for nothing and yet for everything. In all my life I have never felt this small, this devastated; the cell is so dismal that I miss my mother, whom I haven't thought about in ages, and I miss my father too, though I've thought about him even less. And I miss Ajshe too, her serenity; she would survive a night like this far better than me, she would be able to remain calm and say exactly the right words to keep herself from losing her mind.

Then the lights are switched off and I hear a lock turn, the fading echo of footsteps. It makes me remember the war years, the days and nights that Ajshe and I spent in front of the television or radio. Those moments that disquiet stole from us, those moments when we were watching the news, one story more desperate than the last, the taste of iron in our mouths, and whenever someone died, whenever a bomb exploded, a house burned down, a building, a village, whenever a gun went off, the silence between us was god stepping into the room. And then we prayed to him, to the god in our house far from home, the god we barely believed in anymore, we asked him, *please, save the two of us, let that body be someone else's sister, someone else's father, brother, cousin.*

And when he finally replied to our prayers and saved us, and someone else's sister was violently raped, someone else's brother was murdered, unfamiliar villages were razed to the ground, we felt relieved, lighter somehow, if only for a moment, and Ajshe asked, do you think we are bad people, you and I, for hoping and thinking and feeling things like this?

I couldn't answer her, because I didn't know what was acceptable or natural to feel during a war. But I guess it's one thing to hope these things don't happen to you and another to wish them on other people.

This continued for weeks, months, years after the war had ended. Regret caught in the throat, rose up to the mouth like potent bile, its taste wouldn't go away, and guilt took hold of the eyes, making everything its slave, and god wouldn't leave our house either but wandered from room to room in the air that flowed through the apartment, he hid behind our belongings concealed in cupboards, lurked between the sheets and inside a newly acquired dishwasher, left his role as answerer of prayers and turned into questions we asked ourselves every day in front of the mirror but never dared ask each other.

During that time, how could Ajshe concentrate on what our children were saying, on cooking dinner, cleaning, constantly washing laundry and scrubbing the bathroom? How did she have the energy to open her mouth, get dressed, and take a shower? How did she have the strength to answer their endless questions?

On one occasion Ajshe heard that her cousin had given birth in the middle of the woods, where she and her family had fled. "She lost a lot of blood," Ajshe said. "But she'll be fine, the Serbs will never find them in the woods, they'll never get their hands on that child."

At times I was envious of her and felt a sense of inferiority at being unable to act in the way she did. I often wondered whether she behaved like this out of sheer lack of emotion or because it was easier to feign indifference, to wake up in the morning, go about her chores, and go to bed lying to herself that what was happening in our homeland wasn't really true, that it was happening somewhere far beyond these walls, to the people we no longer were. Perhaps she was so tired of violence that she'd become immune to it, that witnessing and experiencing it no longer felt like anything at all.

When I start to feel tired I lie down, wait for the right words, and invite god to my side, because it's at moments like this that god is supposed to come. But after I have said the few phrases I know to him, he doesn't come to me after all and I am alone, but it doesn't make me too sorrowful. Maybe I've forgotten how you're supposed to pray. Or made the mistake of longing for something I have always lived without.

But I still have a lot to wait for, thirteen months to do what ever I want, thirteen months completely to myself. The more I think about it, the more right it feels, the better and brighter the future appears. This is how this was supposed to go, I reason with myself, and the shock of being sent to prison and the thought of my future deportation begin to recede, like an old man making way for his son.

I have more than a year to plan my life, and after that I will return to Pristina, and then I will find him, this is my final thought, I will spend this night here and tomorrow I will sleep somewhere else, and the day after tomorrow I will be closer to him, to the life I want, and before that I can write and write and write, about my mother and father's life, which was a celebration, or so I've been told, about my children and Ajshe too, about that summer and the following autumn when we first came here, the vast amounts of paperwork we had to fill out, about Kosovo and Serbia and the war, Yugoslavia, Tito, about televisions and radios that we only dared switch on in dark, hushed rooms.

That night I dream about snakes: We are still living in Kosovo, Ajshe is pregnant and sick with cancer, and I drive her to the house of an old woman who has accidentally discovered a cure. The woman had been pickling cabbage when, without her noticing, a small snake wriggled into the preserving jar and suffocated inside it. For weeks it leached its poison into the vinegar water. Preserved cabbage and its brine, *rasoj,* was a great delicacy for the woman's gravely ill husband, and the woman wanted to please him by serving it with every meal. To everyone's astonishment, the man's condition improved significantly over the next months, until he was free of cancer. A miracle, declared the doctor who had been treating him. Then one morning, as she was scooping the last remains of the cabbage onto her plate, the woman noticed the decayed baby viper dangling from her fork.

But as Ajshe and I arrive, the forest around the old couple's house begins to burn, someone, or something, has set it aflame, and we have very little time to find the woman. But then she runs out into the yard shouting in panic upon hearing the howl of a fire-breathing *kulshedra,* she shrieks that we are all going to die, it has torn the sky open and will kill us all, and Ajshe and I hurry back inside the car and drive off, and it moves achingly slowly, almost at a crawl, and screaming people run onto the road, burning alive, and I am forced to drive over them, and the fire is on our heels, licking our toes and singeing our hair, hunting us down, then Ajshe goes into labor and she is in so much pain that she sounds like a flock of cawing crows, and then it pushes its way out, not a baby but a snake, fully grown, flayed and furiously hissing, and Ajshe faints, and I wake up just before it lunges at me from Ajshe's footwell and sinks its fangs into my neck.

1 DECEMBER 2000

I met the man quite often, he was a doctor, a heart surgeon to be
precise. He took me to restaurants and cafés and museums and gave me
pocket money as he might his child, and before long he rented a studio
apartment for me to use in downtown Belgrade.

The building was in a busy block, and there was a bakery opposite
where the same people went in and out every day, the smell of
fresh bread and the clink of the cash register carried right up to my
apartment on the third floor.

I had a kitchenette and a mattress on the floor and some of the man's
old clothes, they smelled of onion, of the man the doctor hadn't been
for a long time. The room was dark and it was lonely there, though he

visited me constantly, after work he would arrive with the weight of
the day on his shoulders, dead with fatigue, the patients' and relatives'
sorrow on his mind, and I thought there is nothing more noble than
a concerned doctor and it was my job to push his weariness aside, to
flush his worries down the drain, to be useful and good to him so that
he would have the strength to get up again in the morning, to care, to
heal, to revive, to operate.

Sometimes when his wife and children were out of town, he invited
me to his home, a two-story detached house on the banks of the Danube.
Sometimes I even spent the night there. It was the most beautiful place
I'd ever seen, a fabled land.

I loved him, god how I loved him, he was perfect and bulky and hairy
as a gorilla. I made love with him, caressed him, massaged him, I did
whatever he asked of me because he never forced me to do anything, that
was the best of all, I licked his armpits and groin all over, he liked that
and he liked me and I liked the fact that he liked it, and of course I liked
him too. He resembled my father.

What do you want to do with your life, he once asked me, and I
couldn't answer him, and I was ashamed that I hadn't given a thought
to life after him, it was stupid, of course, spectacularly so, because the
war was already knocking on our doors, waiting in locked basements
and dark alleys, shaking hands with men in suits.

I am leaving Serbia, I can't bear watching this never-ending feud
any longer, he informed me, and I collapsed because now I knew for
sure that one day he would no longer be there, I'm going to Denmark,
I'm going to start working at a hospital there, he told me, and I cried

against his sturdy chest saying, please stay, please please don't leave, don't ever leave, and again he said, hey, kiddo, in that familiar way he had, tell me what you want to do with your life, I need to know because I'll be leaving soon, and all that came out of my mouth was I want to be just like you, that's right, exactly like you.

Is there anything else you'd like to do, he asked, running his rough fingers along my back. No, there's nothing else, I assured him and cried some more, I wanted to sink my nails into his back, transform myself into his skin or one of his eyes, will you take me with you, I heard myself ask, and he said it would be impossible, you know that, you know why, yes, I said, yes I suppose I do.

Kiddo, he said again, kiddo, kiddo, the word steamed from his mouth, in that case I'll make a few phone calls, okay, but you can't tell anyone about me or about us, he said firmly, you can never tell anyone about me, about us, ever, and I said of course I wouldn't tell anyone, not under any circumstances, never ever, that much I can promise you, we can never talk about this to anyone because nobody would understand, isn't that right, and the next day, after making a few calls, he told me I would be starting medical studies in Pristina the following autumn, did you hear that, at the University of Pristina, there's a little apartment there ready for you too.

At that I started laughing at him and I suppose there must have been a touch of mockery in my laughter because the idea was so ridiculous, you can't become a doctor just like that, especially not someone like me, I told him and shook my head, then he gripped me and shouted, KIDDO, you can be whatever you want to be, there's room

in this world for all kinds of doctors, remember that, you can become
anything at all, he held my head in place with his enormous hands, be
hardworking and don't give up, he said urgently, and that moment, he
said, the moment that at first seems impossible, you know when you're
convinced there's nothing to be done, you've experienced it, haven't
you, he asked and I dutifully nodded because I had experienced it many
times, that's the best moment, he said, the BEST, believe it, I've seen
it in sick people and in healthy people, in myself and those close to me,
faced with death a person is as close to the radiance of life as can be—
remember this when you're ready to give up, because then you really
are at your best; a lack of options is in fact a multitude of possibilities.

Promise me that you'll go to Pristina, he said, his hands still cupped
round my head as if it were a chestnut.

say it, he insisted, and I said very well and cried some more and some
more, I'm sorry

don't apologize, but say after me, "I will be a doctor," and so I said I
will be a doctor

say after me, "I am hardworking," and so I said that too, I am
hardworking, I am hardworking

promise me you'll never tell anyone about yourself or about us, about
who I am or who you are, promise you'll keep yourself to yourself and
not cause trouble or prompt the wrong kinds of questions, that you

won't make a spectacle of yourself, you know this but I'll say it anyway
just to be sure, kiddo, don't trust anybody, do your exams, promise me,
promise, and I sobbed that I promise you all these things, very well,
I will go to Pristina I will be a doctor I promise

I love you, the words echoed in the room, and it didn't matter which of
us said it because those words were true—

and then he released his grip on me and left, and I never saw him again,
but he accompanied me everywhere, a divine presence, he was there
in the documents he gave me, in the handwriting on my new school
certificates, in the scent that never fades from his clothes

I thought I would never meet anyone like him again but
then I met you

9

The prison is massive and modern. It reminds me of a large, sleeping octopus; the buildings surrounded with electric fencing are like tentacles extending out from the watchtower. In my ten-square-meter cell there is a window that can be opened, and though there are concrete bars in front of it at least it means I can air the cell and bring in the smell of the rain and forests. I have a bed, a desk, a toilet cubicle with a sink and a small cupboard for hygiene products, and I learn that if I behave well, I might even get a television. A television!

I am given a sack containing dark gray clothes, sweaters and T-shirts, pants, shoes, sandals, socks and underpants, sheets, a toothbrush—nothing excessive. They also give me a set of plastic cutlery and a lunchbox with a lid.

We fetch food from the kitchen and eat in our cells, not all together, as I had imagined. It's best like this, I think as I eat my first meal, rice with chicken sauce, so that the inmates don't spend too much time with one another, plotting things together. The next day we have potatoes and ground-beef sauce, on the third day soup with toasted bread, on the fourth pasta with sauce.

Wake-up is at six a.m., breakfast usually consists of porridge, sandwiches with sliced sausage and cheese, and coffee, and after that we start work at seven. I work in the laundry. It's simple, easy work. We wash the prisoners' clothes and sheets, then place the cleaned items in numbered bags that the prisoners collect at the end of the day. We have lunch at eleven, after which we return to work for a while.

At three p.m. we have two hours' free time; we can go outside into the yard, play table tennis, football, or basketball, even go to the gym. Then it's time for our evening meal, and after that the cell doors are locked at around eight p.m., to wait until the next morning when it will all start over again. The days are so similar that after a while you can barely tell them apart.

All this aside, the place isn't so bad, and it's hard to imagine that it's a prison at all because the conditions are significantly more pleasant than the place where Ajshe and I spent months as refugees after our years in Pristina, and far nicer than the bleak reception center where we spent our first year in this country—here we can have hobbies, we can work, spend time together, and we have more than enough food.

The guards trust us, they take us at our word, and scuffles are rare because everybody seems content. I never hear anyone complaining about maltreatment, and only rarely does anyone express discontent out loud. Longing is mostly reserved for children and wives and parents waiting at home, and hardly ever for freedom, for going to amusement parks or the movies, going for walks in the woods or the park, visiting restaurants or driving around in the car, though many people probably miss these things too.

To Ajshe, however, I say the exact opposite: *don't come here, it's terrible, I don't want you to see me in a place like this, I don't want you to have memories from here,* and so she never visits me. She assures me that the children believe the lies she has told them about me. On the phone she sounds relatively relaxed, repeating the same words of comfort, though I sense she knows that my expressions of concern aren't genuine, that in the words we send each other along the phone lines there is the same distance that has always existed between us, large enough to fit an ocean. I call her during the initial months after my sentencing, then the calls dry up altogether.

The inmates here don't seem to consider their time in prison humiliating; that's perhaps the greatest surprise to me, as in Kosovo being sent to jail brings profound shame upon the entire family, and the only way to fully shake off that shame is to make a public display of shutting the felon out of the family. The offender's parents generally end up denying their child, he becomes nothing but air, and you cannot talk with him, because you cannot talk with thin air. Instead, people say, *unfortunately he got mixed up with the wrong crowd and ended up in prison, and it's the right place for a scoundrel like that, he will never be forgiven for his deeds, he will have to answer to Allah, the doors of whose kingdom will be eternally shut to him, that is his punishment and it's a good thing too, let the cur burn in hell through all eternity and think about whether it was really worth it.*

In Kosovo, prisons are places where the living wish they were dead. Yet prisoners, once they are released, are unable to return to a normal life and often wish only to go back inside. Though the cells are tiny and cramped, though there's little food and the shower, toilet, and kitchen facilities are dilapidated, and though the guards and the stronger prisoners will eat the weaker ones alive, prison is still a sort of home, because there is no place for a former convict in the outside world where everybody knows your name, your unforgivable deed.

Back there, someone being sent to prison is better off taking their own life. Why suffer in prison first, live in fear of others and among all that havoc only to end up condemned for all eternity? If you kill yourself before going to prison, there is still a chance of forgiveness, maybe god will not consider your crime as reprehensible as the living do, maybe god will see farther, understand why someone was selling drugs or weapons, why they robbed and raped, maybe in someone who commits suicide god can see bravery and self-respect, maybe he will reassess the offender's sentence and in the best scenario release them of their sins.

Here, when the cells are locked for the night the inmates chat out of the windows, share their news and comment on TV shows as though they were part of a reality into which they will return after serving their time. The bars across the windows are far enough apart to fit a packet of cigarettes, the prison's currency, which the prisoners use as stakes when playing chess or table tennis. The inmates use shoes to smuggle items to different floors: the laces are tied together and the shoe is lowered or hoisted from one floor to another.

An elderly man lives in the cell next to me. He and I sometimes talk in the evenings, though I mostly keep myself to myself because I'm not in the mood for conversation. He tells me he has been convicted for fraud.

"Always tell people you were convicted of fraud, it's a running joke in this place," he says, and when I tell him I was convicted of fraud too, he laughs.

"False accounting, right?"

"False accounting."

If you are friendly and respectful toward the other inmates, you are left in peace. You have to be invisible in a way that's natural, that fits your character. If you look as though you're not thinking about anything, you try to blend in with the wallpaper and move around the common areas without looking at other people, you'll get off lightly. I stop smoking too, because I don't want to carry anything around that someone else might want from me. I've been thinking this might be a good principle for everyone: don't own or look like you own anything that someone else might covet. I don't try to get to know the others, I don't have opinions on anything, and I don't take part in the group therapy sessions, anger-management courses, or the traditional barbecue parties. I even pretend to speak their language worse than I really do.

I try to write in the evenings, but it's hard without having anything to read. I don't understand this language well enough to get anything out of reading their books, so I bring up the matter when I visit the prison warden to talk about how my time here is going. It turns out he is himself an avid reader, and when I tell him I used to study literature in Pristina we end up discussing the books we have read and how he always dreamed of studying literature too and writing a book but ended up studying public administration instead.

"That's life," he surmises. "We rarely get to do what we really want."

"That's true," I reply.

"Give me a list of the books you'd like to read, and I'll see what I can do," he says after I complain that the only books in English in the prison library are thrillers and romances.

"Really?" I ask, astonished.

"Absolutely," he replies.

I excitedly write down a list of literary classics. If I give him the impression that I only read books that have changed the world, books from which we can learn something important and educate ourselves, perhaps he will think of me more favorably, perhaps he'll see me as more than just a criminal.

Less than a week later all the books I asked for arrive. *The Tin Drum, The Magic Mountain,* and *Death in Venice, The Stranger, Giovanni's Room,* and *The Picture of Dorian Gray, Crime and Punishment* and *The Hours.*

Though these novels are all somewhat similar, most of them tales of men or boys whose lives are upturned in the most incredible and tragic ways, they bring me a great deal of joy.

After lockdown, I push earplugs deep into my ears and read. Every so often the warden asks what I think about the books, and I tell him I'm enjoying them immensely. I dare not answer honestly and tell him what I really think, how I am envious of those writers, both of their ability to imagine such stories and worlds and their skill at being able to translate those thoughts into written form, into flowing, beautiful, aromatic text, into words wrapping other words inside them, endlessly.

In their words, a writer can live on in the most honorable way. As I read the books that have been brought in especially for me, I can't help but wonder at the time I've wasted these past years, at how little I have read considering how much I enjoy reading.

I try to write something every day, but my sentences feel soulless and the texts I put together don't bring to life someone who could be real, someone with whom a reader might identify, and don't at all conjure up the world I am trying to depict. I try to develop a couple of stories—a soldier in the KLA disguises himself as a Serb; a young boy seeks revenge after witnessing the murder of his parents and plans to take matters into his own hands; a greedy weapons dealer ends up shooting himself—but none of the characters I create speaks to me deeply enough to make me want to tell their story, and what I manage to get down on paper doesn't match the imagination in which I dip my pen.

Instead, I write about myself and my own life as I would a diary. I start with my childhood, my first memories of a time when my greatest worry was being late for school or a meeting with a friend, a time when you take pleasure in life in a way it's impossible to experience as an adult—I write about that incredible ability to let go, to become excited about something and wait impatiently for tomorrow, and the moment when you realize that skill has gone forever.

I write about my youth, when even the smallest adversity felt like the end of the world, a bad grade in geometry class like a slap in the face. I write about the disappointment when, as an adult, you suddenly ask yourself, was this it? How was this life—the world's cruelest lie—so different from the stories that attempt to imitate it, that encourage us to stick it out from one tragedy to the next. For most people, the world is a forest raging with fire; there is more destruction than reconstruction, and although there are more people than ever, somehow there's less life now than before.

Writing isn't particularly liberating, but it helps me kill time and tolerate the loneliness. My notebook doesn't get close to full, though I write in a broad hand that takes up space, about my life, its successes, its losses. My accomplishment, a notebook crumpled around the edges in which entire lives intersect with one another for a few dozen pages, is a pathetic sight.

I once read somewhere that there's a downside to a dream come true, because once it becomes real, the dreamer has given the dream away. It made me pensive, even slightly saddened, because I started to think that people should be afraid of their dreams, especially of them coming true. If the value of dreams is in the dreaming itself, what is a dream worth once it's realized? What value is there in a book, if when it's published it is nothing but a dream that the author has given away?

Amid all of this, I think a lot about Miloš. That feeling when I looked him in the eyes, that curious combination of distance and proximity, the uncertainty about whether he was looking back at me or at something behind me. I wonder what kind of life he is living right now, whether he is working somewhere as a doctor, a surgeon, like he always wanted, or maybe he is running a private clinic, he has his own house, a yard, and a garden only a short walk from the water's edge, everything he always talked about. I think of the way he had of picking up a plate, his pincer-like fingers, that summer and that final night to which I have returned every day since, that I have relived in my mind over and over and over.

I try to imagine the moment I meet him again, we bump into each other by accident in front of his workplace or in the street; I wonder what that moment might be like, the moment when he sees me and I see him again after all these years, do we kiss there and then, in the entrance to the hospital or amid the traffic, would we dare, at the same kind of junction where I first saw him, or do we just hug each other and go somewhere for a quiet coffee, to a restaurant for dinner, and only after that do we go to my place or to his apartment, we take hold of each other as though no time had passed at all, we don't necessarily even talk to each other, we don't let go, and everything between us is taken for granted, written out: he and I in a house that is ours, a place where no one disturbs us, and there is a wide, princely bed where we spend every night together, rooms where, over time, our belongings migrate, spreading out like a metropolis.

I arrived in Pristina one June afternoon years ago. Everything will start in Kosovo, I told myself, here I will be a doctor, I said there at the heart of the trampled city, crushed at the legs.

A doctor.

A surgeon.

A heart surgeon.

The locals were wild and beside themselves . . . the soldiers and their guns and equipment were like drizzle—kill or die, it seemed as if everyone was saying to one another, as though every Serb and every Albanian had sensed what was about to happen, as though even I had known it, known that one day

we kill or we die

. . .

*I walked from the bus station to the address the man had given me,
slowly, as though through a nocturnal jungle, I knocked at the door,
told the Albanian man who opened up my name and showed him the
papers I'd been given. I had never even met an Albanian, at least I'd
never knowingly spoken to one, I'd only heard about them, mostly
hellish stories, and I was so petrified with fear that I was prepared for
anything.*

*I've been expecting you, said the Albanian; it turned out he was
very friendly and immediately beckoned me into his home, which was
beautiful and immense, almost a sibling of the house of the man I loved
and had left in Belgrade, welcome, said the Albanian and asked me to
sit down at a brass table, and I felt like an imposter, an orphan; after
all, that's what I was.*

*The man handed me a stack of papers, which I signed with my
initials M.M., he gave me various documents from the University of
Pristina, then he gave me an envelope and the keys to my future home,
it's very close, he told me, walking distance from the university, it'll be
easy to find your way to lectures.*

*Then the man took me to the apartment, you know where, the one on
the second floor, opposite the bakery, the one that looked like the cell of a
shriveled, forgotten saint. I've given you everything that was agreed, he
said, remember to be careful round here, a Serb in an Albanian mosque,
and when he left, the apartment shrank into a cage trapping a tiger cub
away from its mother.*

Nobody knows anything about me unless I tell them myself,

I thought that first night, and I was about to lose my mind, this is an awful place and city, poor and diminutive, I thought the following night and shouted into my pillow, but the third night, and the fourth, and all the nights after that were easier, more gentle, and I dreamed a lot: in one dream there were tigers dotted across a town square, languidly taking in the sun as the people looked on; in another they prowled the streets, erratically smashing windows, pulling up bushes and plants in frustration and wildly breaking locks; in a third they fomented terror by frightening children for the sheer malicious joy of it.

I opened the envelope, which was full of money. With it was a note in which the man asked me to promise the things I had already promised him, is he still going on about these things, I wondered as I folded the note and slid it back into the envelope, because I have already moved far away from him, and he even farther from me; he didn't know the conniving brute that would become of me here.

10

2004

I am told I will be released a few months early due to good behavior.

A week before the end of my sentence I meet the prison warden for the last time. He asks me how I would like to take care of the practicalities of my deportation. *Does your wife know about this, will she be waiting for you? What about your children, do they know their father is coming home for a while? Do you have any suitcases to pack up your things? Did you know you can take two large suitcases with you and one piece of hand luggage? Do you have an apartment in Kosovo, somewhere to stay? What about work? Or money, then?*

I feel bad having to say no to almost every question. I avoid eye contact with him, and the only thing I'd like to tell him is that I would rather go straight to the airport. I am ashamed, my clothes feel disgusting, damp and warm.

"This must be very difficult," he says sympathetically.

"I'll return the books," I manage to say.

"You can take them with you if you want," he says and clears his throat.

"No, I can't take them," I reply.

"Yes, you can, with my permission," he tells me.

"I'm sorry, but they are very heavy and I don't have enough room for them," I reply. "But it's a kind thought."

"Very well."

Then he informs me that my flight via Budapest to Pristina will depart the next day and that I will be driven home to pack before that.

"That's how I have arranged things," he says.

"Thank you."

"So you might want to let your wife know," he then says pointedly, as though he knows I haven't told Ajshe anything.

"Yes."

After this, the warden explains, I will be transported to the police station, where I will spend one night, after which two plainclothes police officers will escort me all the way to Pristina, they will fly with me and set me free only once we have landed. It seems a bit over-the-top, because there's no way I could possibly escape while we're ten kilometers in the air, and I almost feel like asking whether I could travel alone, without giving outsiders the chance to speculate as to why I am being escorted—it would only frighten the other passengers, especially the children. In my mind I promise him I won't try anything, that I will return to Pristina in a spirit of cooperation.

"Good," I reply instead and take a deep breath.

My hands begin to sweat, and then, all of a sudden, I slump, powerless, a limpness spreading through my body like the taste of spicy food through my mouth, while I try to do everything I can to retain my posture. The warden hands me a tissue, which I use to hide my wet face and press against my eyes, and it's as if there's no end to the trickle of tears welling from them.

"Oh dear," says the warden. "I'm sorry."

"No," I mumble from behind my fingers. "I am sorry. Thank you," I continue and reveal my swollen, red, throbbing face.

"It's all right," says the warden. "I'm sure this must be difficult."

"I . . . I could take the books after all."

"Good," he replies and stands up from behind his desk, then I stand up too, and he walks in front of me and offers me his hand, which I grip, pulling him closer, turning his handshake into a half embrace, which then turns into a kiss that I place on his right cheek.

He pushes me away slightly, stares at me in bewilderment for a moment, then lowers his eyes to my cheeks and lips, and at that his expression changes and becomes more serious, and after this he looks me in the eyes again, my eyes gleaming just as his do, and eventually he kisses me on the right cheek too.

As I step through our front door, Ajshe looks at me as though I were a ghost. It is a mid-spring morning and there is a chill in the air, and she is wearing an apron; her eyes look ridiculously large, her tongue is numb, it rests at the bottom of her open mouth like a dead eel, her dry hands, white as paper, on her bony hips.

"Is it really you?" she stammers as I take off my shoes.

"Hello, Ajshe," I say mundanely, though I almost burst at the sight of her; my home is clean, the smell of food and freshly laundered clothes brings to mind those quiet, shared mornings when the children had already gone to school and we could bury ourselves in the languid slumber of our everyday for a while. "I have to go."

I walk past her into the bedroom, and the first thing I do is unpack the books I got from prison and pile them on Ajshe's bedside table. From the closet I take the old suitcases, the ones we packed our belongings in after we fled Kosovo and came here, and place them on the neatly made bed. My clothes, my underpants, my socks, everything has been washed, ironed, and folded.

As I place my clothes into the suitcases—for some reason I am in a terrible hurry, though I should have plenty of time, at least that's what I've been told—Ajshe, standing in the doorway, begins to whimper.

"Ajshe," I say. "Please."

"This is terrible," she whispers, holds a hand across her mouth, glances quickly at the helpless-looking men still standing in the hallway, wipes her cheeks, and takes a deep breath.

"Very well," she says, steps to my side, and grips my trembling hand.

The walls are white and unadorned; trapped in a white throw our bed looks like a polar bear in winter sleep, and the light brown curtains descend from the rail like two men dangling from the gallows.

"Let me," she insists, and I almost forget to tell her something important, my wish that she give the books to the children when they grow up as gifts from me, then she pulls me with her into the kitchen, where she sits me down and begins preparing an omelette, which is before me on the table complete with accompaniments within five minutes.

"Eat," she commands, strokes my hair, and disappears from the kitchen, and as I begin to chew I can hear Ajshe plumping up my clothes in the bedroom, quietly singing a song—I can't make out the words—and as she packs my belongings I imagine her picking up each piece, touching every single shirt, every sock, gripping them the way she used to hold my hand.

Twenty minutes later Ajshe carries the packed suitcases into the hallway and marches back into the kitchen. She is not the same person as a moment ago; her eyes are bulging feverishly now, her lips taut as though she has just bitten into a bitter fruit. She sits down opposite me.

"I'll tell them that you have gone, that you have left us," Ajshe begins sternly. "My sister and Besnik, everyone. That's what I'll tell them," she continues, unflinching, and I stare at the empty plate in front of me.

"Ajshe," I interrupt—and there is so much I want to say to her, I want to apologize for everything, tell her this is all my fault, that I have broken us, that the shame you feel toward me is completely justified and is nothing compared to the humiliation into which I have driven myself and that will eventually take everything from me, my face, my honor—but she doesn't give me the chance to say anything.

"And if anyone asks you about us, you will answer in the same way. Right?"

"Yes."

"I will get married again, if I want to. To a foreign man. Or a Kosovan. Or whomever I wish. Is that clear?"

"Yes."

She would never dare set out demands like this if we were alone. Then she takes an envelope from her pocket and lays it on the table. She places a finger on the envelope and slides it in front of me. "There is half of our savings."

"Ajshe," I say again, and she pulls herself farther away from me.

"You can have it, but on the condition that you promise never to tell anyone the truth about what you did, about what you are, I heard what you did and who you did it with, you raped that poor boy, didn't you, that's what everyone's saying, and it disgusts me," she whispers through clenched teeth, her eyes almost translucent, and lifts her finger from the envelope.

Then she stands up, takes the plate from in front of me, and hurls it into the sink, and the sound of the shattering plate is almost like a ringing phone.

"*Dreqi të hangt!*" she shouts, gripping the edge of the sink and collapsing in inconsolable wailing, and it's as though she were about to split in two; her slender back drops and hunches as she sobs in fits, her legs dangle limp from her hips as though she is holding her entire body weight with only her arms.

I stand up, slip the envelope into my pocket, and step behind her, I grip her shoulder, but she flicks my hand away instantly.

"Don't touch me!" she shouts, lowering her face toward the sink, and at that the men come running into the kitchen.

"Everything all right, madam?" one of them asks her while the other looks at me as though I were an angry, unleashed dog.

"Yes," Ajshe replies, and wipes her face clean with a sheet of kitchen paper, and I begin walking toward the hallway, pull on my shoes, grip the suitcases.

"Ajshe," I say once more, and a moment later she appears in front of me, takes off her apron, and hangs it on a hook.

At first her arms are folded across her chest, then they point toward me, and a few cautious steps later they wrap around me as around a precious vase.

"Thank you," I say and notice a tear or a droplet of my sweat soaking into her cotton sweater, and I hear one of the men clearing his throat.

"Goodbye," Ajshe says, whimpering, lowers her arms, and retreats toward the kitchen doorway. "Goodbye, Arsim," she says once again, this time more emphatically; her gaze is piercing. "Take care of yourself."

The door closes, and I enter the silent stairwell, walk down the stairs, the corners of the suitcases knocking against them, then another door opens, and it leads outside into a day that smells like my wife's hair and an opened freezer, into the pale spring sunshine that ripples through the nearby forest in a wave whose kaleidoscopic waters glide inland like a giant stingray rising up into the mountains, washing their scarred backs.

12 DECEMBER 2000

*THINK ABOUT THIS IT MAKES ME FEEL BETTER
SOMETIMES:*

> *one day we will leave here*
> *one day we will all leave*
> *and we will fly there*
> *wild*

The Devil locked God's daughter and the snake together in one of the caves inside his mountain.

"First eat the cockroaches, the moths, the spiders, and the scorpions, then the rats, and bats, the foxes and wolves, and give half of each meal to the girl," the Devil instructed his snake, which was thrashing in horror. "I will come to you once a year, on Saint George's Day, to make sure you are doing as I have advised you," he explained, hurled the viper dangling from his hand at the rough cave wall and glanced over at the girl, sleeping calmly, whom he had wrapped in beeswax. "And when the last wolf's bone has been licked clean, one of you will eat the other," the Devil decided.

In the thirteenth year, the Devil was met by the most astonishing sight he had ever laid eyes upon: the girl had now become one with her prey, clothed in a magnificent snake skin, in winged majesty, both the girl and the snake living from the darkness and each other.

"Bolla," said the Devil and allowed the sun to shine in through the mouth of the cave, to light his creation.

Then the girl felt sunlight for the first time, and it was beautiful.

11

The years away from here condense into a flicker as I step through the doors of Pristina airport. In the early-evening April light, the valleys around me look like a smoker's withered lungs, and throughout the taxi journey into the city's heart I stare in bewilderment at the buildings, many of which look as though a merciless whirlwind has torn off their roofs and kicked down their walls, leaving only the foundations among which the people now live; I look at the dust hanging in the air, the streets full of potholes half filled with black, oily water, billboards propped in the gravel and blown askew in the wind, mountains that look like imams in their *sarëk* headdress, crouched in prayer, the edges of the fields where burned litter has clawed at the bone-dry earth.

I arrive downtown, and carrying my suitcase I walk along the only pedestrian street in Pristina, sit down on a bench, and light a cigarette.

It tastes really good, my first cigarette in months, the smoke seeps inside me, cool and minty, but after a moment I feel faint, the smoke and all the people I see, the language they speak, the way they are dressed, the surprising number of women covering their heads, how people buy food from miserable-looking, tiny convenience stores, then pack it in small plastic bags that tear in your hands. This place is a prison, far worse than the one I have just left.

I spend the night at a cheap hotel near the center of town. I switch on the lights in the room tinted with a wine-red bedspread, an olive-green carpet, and a set of brown curtains. I sit down on the edge of the bed but immediately spring up again and switch off the lights; I close the curtains and allow shame and regret to do their job: to crush my insides, to batter my head against the floor and ceiling, to repeat those unconditional words tumbling from the wall of night, the ones we say to ourselves at the worst moments, the ugliest words that we only dare speak out loud while the rest of the world is sleeping.

It is the most barbaric night of my life, the kind I wouldn't wish upon even the worst of men.

The following day is baking hot, and in the afternoon I arrive at my former home in Ulpiana, my palms blistered from carrying my suitcases and my clothes soaked in sweat. I cautiously step into the stairwell, leave the suitcases in the soot-covered entrance hall, and walk up the familiar stairs to the door of our old apartment, which is new and now has three locks.

The sound of footsteps comes from behind the door, and in front of it there is a mat wishing me welcome, two pairs of plastic sandals, a pair of children's sneakers, and black leather shoes, torn at the seams. My head is starting to ache and I knock stiffly at the door; my palms feel like there are worms moving around inside them and my mouth is dry as sandpaper.

"Who's there?" comes a low, serious voice from behind the door.

I say nothing; instead I knock again.

"Who's there?" comes the question again, then I hear a woman's voice, quiet and panicked, speaking the man's name.

Bashkim.

"Bashkim," I begin. "Stop messing around, it's me. Open the door."

The man is big, determined, and angry looking. Beneath his tall, wide brow, I can barely make out his threatening eyes, which look as though they have been walled shut. I stare at his face, at once jaundiced and ruddy, his hands dotted in a patchwork of calluses, his suit pants, threadbare at the knee, his bare feet covered in scratches, his cracked toenails, then my gaze returns to his eyes, which now I can see better.

"Who are you?" the man asks.

"This . . . ," I begin and swallow too much air. "This is my apartment," I manage to say, correcting my posture and pushing my rib cage forward.

The man folds his arms and assumes a wider gait so that he fills the doorway, and his eyes retreat, while his brows form into a single, hairy strip.

"I've fought in the war," he says. "I'm not afraid of guns, prison, or Allah, but I will defend my family," he continues sternly, as unflinching as a bodyguard.

Then a woman appears behind him and casts a fiery look at me; she is carrying a baby wrapped in a towel and holding a preschool-aged boy by the hand.

"I bought this door," the man says. "And everything else you can see. After the war there was nothing here, the walls were covered in graffiti, the floors ripped up, only the pipes left in the kitchen. In the bathroom there was nothing but debris and a pungent, unpleasant smell."

"You are living in my apartment," I interject firmly, though I believe the man's words, though I know and accept that the apartment, which once was my home, is no longer my home, that it will never be my home again.

"I live here, this is my apartment now," the man declares and slams the door shut, and not a sound comes from behind that door for the five minutes I stand in the corridor before turning and walking back down the stairs.

I take my suitcases to a café, order a coffee, watch the people walking past me, eat the sugary cookie wrapped in thin plastic that comes with it. There was a time when men shot each other if they stole from each other, I think to myself, but that time is in the past, and I'm not sure whether it's more a good or a bad thing.

As I listen to a group of girls cackling with laughter at the next table, it dawns on me how pathetic I am. It's a thought that's hard to swallow: to have once been so many things—a student, a writer, a father, husband, and companion—and suddenly so little, nothing at all.

I pull my phone from my pocket and dial Ajshe's number, as I am consumed by an abrupt need to tell her about all this, our occupied apartment, the ubiquitous smell of meat and frying fat, the Albanian they now speak here, which is somehow different from the way we speak it, the grime and dust and dampness that have enveloped the streets, the jewelers, the clothes shops and seamstresses and kiosks and general stores, whose clutter spills out into the streets making the whole city look like a dump— even the fact that many Chinese entrepreneurs have moved here and opened up shops, and I can almost see the confusion on Ajshe's face: why on earth would someone from China come and open a business here?

A small boy walks up to me. He is carrying the bottom of a cardboard box in which he has organized packets of cigarettes and prepaid cards for local phone operators. I buy two packs of cigarettes and ask where his parents are, and the boy tells me that his father has died and his mother is ill, and I don't know which feels worse to me: the fact that he is selling cigarettes on the street or that I doubt the veracity of his story.

I can't think what words to use to talk about all this—should I greet her at the beginning of the call or apologize or ask how she is—so I slide the phone back into my pocket.

The waiter, a swarthy young man barely out of high school, asks if I'd like to order anything else. I give him a fifty-cent coin for the coffee, then put a five-euro note in his hand.

"You'll get another two of these this evening when I pick up my things," I promise, looking down at my shabby suitcases, which contain everything I own.

"Right," he says, nods, and grips their scuffed handles.

"There's nothing valuable in them, old clothes, two sets of sheets, a few towels, shoes, and some papers I'm not going to do anything with. Have a look, if you want."

"Right," he repeats. "Don't worry, *zotëri*, I'll be here until closing. If you don't see me, ask at the counter. My name is Naim."

"Good," I reply, stand up, and offer him my hand. "Thank you, Naim."

First off, I visit Miloš's apartment, but where it stood there is no longer a residential house but a poky hotel. Disappointed, I walk off toward the city center, past the café where we first met, and when I notice that in its place there is now an empty retail space, to my surprise I'm almost relieved and continue on my way, past the National Library, which still looks like a cluster of wasps' nests, past the Faculty of Philosophy, a building resembling an industrial warehouse, past the entire campus area, covered in uneven lawn. Again I arrive at the only pedestrian street in the city, at the end of which is the National Theatre of Kosovo, its steps leading down into Mother Teresa Square. Standing in the middle of the square, the statue of Skanderbeg on horseback looks, from afar, more like a muddy raven's claw rising from the ground than a depiction of our national hero. At the end of the street, I turn right because I want to go for a walk in the City Park, but just before the entrance a white sign in front of one of the houses offering a small room for rent catches my eye.

The tin-roofed building is old and crooked, and the windows that open out onto the busy street are small and rickety, but nonetheless I call the number on the sign.

A man quickly answers. I introduce myself using just my first name and get straight to the point. In an absentminded voice, he tells me he lives there himself and that he'll be at home for a little while yet, so if I want to, I can come look at the room right away.

A few minutes later he steps out of the house's metal gates and glances around; he is gaunt and hunched, his movements exhibiting the same kind of indifference as someone terminally ill, and from his ringless fingers, his unshaved jowls, his disheveled hair and oversized, badly fitting clothes one can tell he has nobody to look after him, to make sure he doesn't waste away further still.

As I cross the street, the man sees me and gives a cautious smile. He has only a few teeth, and even they are cracked and covered in black spots.

"I'm Behxhet, how do you do?" he says over the noise of

the street and limply holds out his hand, and as I grip it I feel
as though we two were cut from exactly the same cloth, grown
from the same root.

"Arsim. I'm well. Yourself?"

"Fine, fine."

His tired eyes stand lazily in their sockets, and his cheeks and
forehead dangle like hand towels on a clothesline.

We descend a few steps to an unpaved outdoor corridor giving private access to both rooms. Between the doors, against my
wall, is an old stove, and on the open shelf above it is a collection
of dishes and plastic containers, packets of tea and coffee, canned
food, a sack of white beans, and a bag of overripe tomatoes. On
the ground is a breadbasket, a few buckets, and a hose winding its
way into a shower cubicle, which is also outdoors and cordoned
off with a curtain. The toilet is in a tin shack in a small garden, in
which is the same plastic dining set that can be found all over the
place here, a round white table and three chairs, one of which is
missing a leg.

"I live over here," says the man and indicates the door to his
own room, looking down at the sandals next to it. "And this
room is for rent," he continues, turns his head in the other direction, and sticks his forefinger and middle finger into his pocket to
pull out a heavy key ring.

He opens the door, and the smell of wet wood surges out of
the apartment. I step inside; the room is dark and damp, like the
mouth of someone out of breath, the floor is covered in brown
patterned carpet, and in front of the windows is a set of curtains in a matching shade of brown, in one corner stands a wob-
bly chest of drawers and in the other a chair brought in from
the yard, in front of which is a small desk. In the middle of the
room is an old wooden sofa bed, its mattress covered in stains and
spatter.

"This'll be a hundred euros a month," he informs me from the corridor, and I turn and look at him standoffishly.

"I'll pay seventy euros, you can have the first month up front and the next month's rent on the final day of the previous month."

"Eighty-five," he says. "This is downtown."

"Seventy. Otherwise I'll walk right out of here."

"Seventy euros," the man repeats and closes his eyes, as though disappearing for a moment into calculations of everything he could do with that sum of money. It's a lot round here. "Very well. Seventy it is," he finally agrees.

I turn my back to take two notes out of my wallet, then turn around and hand them to him.

"Thank you," he says and stuffs the notes into his back pocket, takes two keys from the key ring, and drops them in my hand.

I don't stay to look around but go back to the café to pick up my belongings. The familiar waiter is sitting at a table in the empty café and appears happy to see me. He fetches my suitcases and I give him the money I promised. On the way back to the house, the suitcases no longer seem to weigh anything. I empty them, put my things in the chest of drawers and the closet, then wrap the mattress, the covers, and pillows in quality foreign sheets. They still smell of the detergent Ajshe always preferred, lavender and vanilla.

I sit down at the little desk and call Ajshe. I don't feel nervous until the phone starts ringing; at the sound of the first ring I spit out the glob of phlegm that has suddenly formed in my throat, by the second ring my heart is beating frantically and my entire body starts to tremble, by the third I find it hard to hold the phone in place at my ear, and by the fourth ring I know she's not going to answer, and then the call is connected to the answering machine where I leave a message, wondering whether these might be the last words I ever say to her.

"Hi. I've arrived safely and I'm doing fine."

For the first few weeks I barely leave my room. I keep the curtains closed and lie on the bed. I sleep, wake up, sleep, drink some water, try to eat some cookies and potato chips, and occasionally I drag myself to the store to buy canned goulash, coffee beans, and fresh white bread that goes moldy before I manage to eat it all. When I realize I don't have a coffee mill, I feel frustrated and throw the coffee beans in the trash, and for a moment everything feels pointless, wasted.

I start to stink. I start to deteriorate. I start hearing voices, words whispered in my ear in different languages, taps at the window, children shouting, scratching sounds beneath the bed. At times they sound like human voices, at others like animals, and all at once I'm sure there is a tall, skinny figure standing in the corner of the room looking at me, but then it turns out to be the wardrobe, the chair, or the clothes draped over its back. Sometimes I even talk to it, and I greet it first then ask it to leave, and it obeys me, slides beneath the carpet or seeps out through the gaps in the window frame.

Behxhet leaves early in the morning and returns at eight in the evening, quickly prepares himself some food, and locks himself in his room, watches television for a few hours until he falls asleep, then the cycle starts over again. I feel exhausted by his daily routine, at how similar each day is, the same meals, the same TV shows, the same clothes, every single day.

I cry in the mornings, I cry during the day, I cry in the evenings and at night, on my way to the park opposite, on the park bench and as I cross the street on the way home, I can't make it stop. I visit the store, I cry there too, I buy a coffee mill, rummage in the trash for the coffee beans I threw away, and enjoy a cup of coffee, but the day after that I don't get out of bed until the evening, and the next day, and the next.

It takes a while before I get used to the lack of things to do, the absence of human touch, before I understand where I am living, before I stop shouting through the nightmares or fumbling at the air when I wake up at the spot where I imagine Ajshe or my children to be.

One evening, Behxhet knocks on my door, and I realize it must be the last day of the month. When I open the door, he looks at me from head to toe, baffled.

"I'm a bus driver," he begins and gives me a toothless smile. "The company is looking for someone to drive another route. You know how to drive a bus?"

"Yes," I answer instinctively, though I've never driven a bus in my life, but I have to start doing something because before long my savings will run out.

"Good. Tomorrow morning, you come with me," he informs me and lays a hand on my shoulder as though I were an old friend. "You'll need to clean yourself up a bit first," he says and turns to the door.

That evening I wash myself, cut my nails, brush my teeth, and shave; I even change the sheets, wash my laundry, and put my room in order. I'm nervous about the idea of driving a bus; I could bump into anyone, even my old acquaintances. Still, I can tolerate shame and embarrassment far better than idleness. Perhaps this is how I know I am different from these people.

In the morning, we walk a short distance to an office where I meet my new boss. He shakes hands with both of us, sits me down in front of him, and begins explaining the route, from

Vreshta to the city center, past the National Theatre, the university campus, the student housing blocks and Ulpiana, to the hospital and back again.

"Easy, it's a nice, simple route," says the boss. "Behxhet can tell you all the practical things you need to know, but there are two rules here: always be careful and always be on time," he continues, then stands up from behind his desk to show us out of the office.

"Thank you," I say and extend my hand, but he doesn't appear to notice.

I start driving the following week; the old, stiflingly hot little German bus moves heavily but surely, forced to negotiate the bumpy roads, the steep hills, and the stress the thick gravel places on the suspension.

Traveling with me is a young conductor who collects twenty cents from everyone getting on the bus, though he lets people he knows on for free. He talks to me all day about trivial things, I reply merely by nodding or grunting, and I'm thankful he soon learns not to ask me anything. The traffic is aggressive and chaotic: people dodge in and out wherever they can and blow their horns for fun, male drivers shout at pedestrians from behind the steering wheel, wolf whistle at young women, greet their friends by sticking their heads out of the car window, a cigarette balanced between their chapped lips.

The days are drawn out, there are almost no breaks, and the wage is less than two hundred euros per month, plus the few coins that the conductor and I agree to put into our own pockets at the end of the shift. Still, the low wages don't bother me, because sitting behind the wheel of the bus my body is no longer the host of inaction but subject to the cycle of life, and so I smile at the passengers as they step on board, and they thank me as they

leave, I look in the side mirror, shift into first gear, put my foot
on the gas, shift into second, then third, and make my way to the
next stop, and the next and the next, and the one after that, and
I find myself examining all the silhouettes that enter my field of
vision, every person my eyes see.

And one day, after a few weeks of driving the bus, my attention is drawn across the street, it is him, those footsteps, that way
of walking, the position of his arms, the neck, slender as a crane's,
the curvature at the back of his head, the hair on his neck, it's
him, I tell myself and brake suddenly, pull over to the side of
the road, the conductor and passengers complain, and I dash out
of the bus and set off running and catch up with him in front of
the Xhamia e Çarshisë, a mosque with walls that resemble bean
soup, and grip him by the delicate shoulders that suddenly don't
feel like his after all; the man turns, revealing his startled face, I'm
sorry, I say, sorry, I mistook you for someone else, I'm terribly
sorry, *zotëri,* I thought you were someone else, and at this the
man's expression becomes slightly less confused and he wishes me
a nice afternoon, nods, and continues on his way.

I run back to the bus and start driving, and for a while I can't
seem to calm my breathing or worsening sweating, the bus jud-
ders along the road and I forget to stop in the right places, and at
some point the conductor asks, who was that man, was it your
brother or a friend, but I don't answer him, and for the rest of the
day I feel shaken, shivering as though a cloth dipped in freezing
water were wrapped round my neck.

That evening I write Ajshe a letter. It feels more respectful than
a text message or talking to her voicemail, and it's harder to dis-
miss. I fold it, slip it into an envelope, and write out Ajshe's name
and address, lick a stamp, and as the shivering abates I realize that
I must find him, the man I met on these pummeled streets almost
ten years ago, he is here, I know it, alive.

Hi,

When I moved back here I thought I'd never be able to experience happiness again, but today I did—I think I can be happy here. Take care.

A.

You know how they say you have to love yourself before you can love
someone else, feed yourself first and only then feed others, help yourself
first to help others—

   what kind of person has the nerve to say that, who has the gall to
utter words like that

      don't the helpless, the hungry, and the loveless deserve love food and help
      what if you're unable to love yourself what happens then

everybody here says they want to help me—we want to help you we
want to help you we want to help you we want to help make you feel
better, that's what they say every day

what a JOKE to get help now, to feel good in a place like this

they embarrass themselves they should travel back in time

they should have been there in the barn when I was eight years old

and my father said

you are a man now

he handed me a knife

kill that crippled calf can't you see it hobbling

kill it

slit its throat my father shouted

and when I picked up the knife, the calf's mother, tethered to a pole,

started struggling and thrashing and bellowing frantically, I looked

straight at the cow's miserable eyes and IT KNEW and I threw the

knife to the ground and ran into the house I spent more time afraid than

I did not afraid in that house

my father killed that calf, its mother looking on,

and he kept me hungry through the months that followed MEAT IS

NO FOOD FOR COWARDS

he said

and punched me in the mouth

or they should have been there when my friends told me that stupid

kids shouldn't go to school, a boy shouldn't behave like a girl, don't

come back tomorrow don't ever come here again

they should have been there then

or when my brother said he was ashamed of me

or when I was homeless and slept in parks

or when I was at the front and didn't know what pity was

where were they then?

12

I visit the university. I tell the elderly gentleman sitting behind the desk that I am a former student, that my education was interrupted because of the war, and that now I would like to complete my studies, starting this autumn if at all possible. He looks me sternly in the eye and asks whether I have any documentation to prove that I studied there before the war, and when I hand him my old proof of registration and incomplete transcript, the man puts the papers to one side, giving them only a cursory glance, and starts twiddling his thumbs, then slowly scratches his temple.

"Well . . . this will mean a lot of work . . . You'll have to pay another registration fee, have the credits you've already done approved one by one, which you'll have to agree with each professor individually, and so on," he says haughtily.

"I understand," I say, take two bills from my wallet, and place them on the desk in the knowledge that, in addition to the registration fee, there will be enough for him too.

The man slides the bills to his side of the desk and promises to get the paperwork done by next week.

When I fetch the papers, I ask the man about a medical student who studied at the same time, Miloš Micić. Upon hearing the name, the man seems clearly uneasy, grips the edge of the desk, and for a moment remains silent, so I add that this is important, I must find this former student. He shakes his head and scoffs that there are no records of any Serbs.

"I'm sure you know that the university was split into many parts during the war and in the aftermath, and the medical faculty was transferred to Serbia," he says. "All the Serbs, students, teachers, and other university staff, they all left town. The faculty no longer exists, at least not as it was."

"I know."

"So, he studied medicine?" the man asks, his expression taut, his mouth clipped into a thin line, and his eyes crumpled like two raisins. "Why would he have stayed here?"

"Exactly."

"Exactly," he repeats and wipes a chubby palm across his face. "This man could be anywhere, surely you realize that, he could be in Serbia or Montenegro or Bosnia or Croatia or Slovenia, anywhere at all, America, Australia even," he explains.

"*Djalosh*," he says, again wiping his brow. "Young man," he repeats, this time more emphatically. "Just let it go."

During the weeks that follow I visit the city hall, the hospital and health centers, I visit the libraries, the government agencies and ministries, even cafés and restaurants, and everyone I meet—doctors, nurses, officials, waiters, restaurateurs—gives me the same answers. Nobody knows a man by that name. They probably think I have an ulterior motive for trying to find him, to take revenge on him, to exact retribution.

After a while I feel deflated. My days are vapid, their guts and innards lie steaming on the floor of my room as though freshly pulled from a pig, and I can barely drag myself to work. I don't have the energy for anything else, not even for greeting the passengers, I don't care where they are going, whether they pay or not, I don't care about the sounds around me, and before long my environment stops offering them to me altogether.

On the way home one evening, I see a secondhand television on sale for next to nothing outside an electronics store, and when the owner assures me it still works and says I can pay half up front and the other half once I've tried it, we shake hands on the deal.

I start following a Turkish drama series telling the story of two feuding families and watch the news, which features the same issues day after day: the rebuilding of the country; the funds received from Europe or America, which will be used to revive the national economy and eradicate unemployment; the struggle for independence; the fight for justice. On the one hand, people want to settle old scores, but at the same time they want to forget the war, to move away from here as quickly as possible, to arrive in the West but still to see their country thriving with investments, with money others have given, work others have done.

Every news story drags behind it a train stained with blood, because everything is always framed through the prism of war: the buildings blasted to the ground will be rebuilt, the bombed roads will be mended, and people will once again find their long-abandoned houses. The Serbs will get what they deserve, they will pay for what they've done.

You can't trust the politicians; they line their pockets with our tax money, appoint their relatives to highly paid govern-

ment positions, everybody knows it's going on, everybody talks
about it, but people vote for the same men at the next election
too because they believe that money will have made these men
replete already, which means they are more likely to build the
schools they promised, open the factories they boasted about,
that's what people say to one another, surely these scumbags have
already stolen more than enough. Maybe on some level the people who vote for these men know that money would make them
just like that too.

The most amusing thing is that after such discussions, people
give thanks to god that the war is now over. I can't understand
how or why people who constantly cheat one another, people
battered by inaction and poverty have fallen for the belief that
there's still hope, that there's still a point in talking about tomorrow though life already happened yesterday, that one day everything will turn out for the best and things will fall into place
because god is great, that's what they say, god is great, god is good.

I sleep, wake up, eat, drive, eat, sleep, and drive again, and I
find it hard to imagine the value of the life I am living. Is there
any sense driving a bus all day long for a wage that barely leaves
me enough for food? Any sense eating out of a can every evening,
living in a moldy house, worrying about freezing when winter
comes and the fact that nobody would miss me if I died—where
is the sense in that? In being alone, living alone? A joyless life
with someone else is always better than a joyless life spent alone.

It's hard not to think about these things because hopelessness
runs through everything here; it's that skinny man over there
wearing a suit and sitting on the street corner, maybe in front of
his store, the old woman crossing the street with a loaf of wheat
bread under her arm, the hungry children and grandchildren
with whom she will soon share it, all those boys begging and
selling cigarettes outside restaurants, the dirty hands stretched

across tables, the wives who disappear into the goldsmith's store to pawn their jewelry.

As the days pass, I begin to think it's increasingly unlikely that I will find him and all the more likely that one day I simply won't get out of bed again. That would be it. The end of a life, at peace with the words spoken and those left unsaid.

There is an item on the news one evening. Foreign journalists have visited a local mental hospital and written pieces published in acclaimed English-language newspapers. The stories allege that people who weren't even sick were being locked up there, and once the war ended even Serbs as punishment for what they did to the Albanians during the war. The journalists say they are calling on international human-rights organizations to take a stand on the matter, as conditions in the hospital are appalling.

Half asleep, I watch the video footage of shaved-headed patients. In the background, an agitated voice explains that starving and emaciated individuals roam the hospital complex as though in a stupor, constantly shouting, begging the few visitors for money, cigarettes, clothes—apparently the advice is not to touch the patients because they have lice, fungal infections, and diseases. There are hardly any decent sanitary facilities, just a few buckets here and there along the corridor; the stench is overwhelming.

The patients masturbate in front of one another, rape one another, and give birth to children who can neither walk nor speak. On television they show a little girl sprawled on a bed; she looks like a drunken spider. They say the patients are constantly being given long-expired medicines, they have no stimuli, nothing to do, they mainly eat *qull,* a porridge made from corn flour, and bread and sleep in turns on the floors lined with excreta because there simply aren't enough beds to go around.

I suppose I should be angry or sad at what I see, I should feel reprehension and disgust, but I don't, and instead I find myself thinking it's a good thing that the Serbs among the patients and prisoners or whatever you decide to call them finally got what they deserved, that now they are finally paying for what they did to this nation, for making our situation what it is today. They haven't been locked up for nothing, I think, and I'm sure many people here think the same, and that's why nothing is done about it. The only thing I wonder about is how any doctor or nurse can work in a place like that and supervise these sick people at such close range.

But then. Then the television screen shows me his face, it is his face, for a few seconds I truly see his face. It is miraculous, like a dream—as though a majestic two-headed eagle had flown into a crowded ballroom and exploded into a shower of money.

He staggers, hunched beneath a sash window, from which just enough light falls on him that I can make out his unfocused gaze, his expression soured with tedium, a flash of his narrow shoulders, his slender arms and bony legs, his brittle hands clasped around his knees.

As the image changes I drop to my knees in front of the television, instinctively clasp its electric edges as though that might bring the image back, might show him again. I'm gasping so hard I can no longer hear the announcer's voice and cannot get up from the floor, though the news bulletin has already moved on to talking about something else.

I fall flat on the floor. I lie there so long that I can feel my cheek assuming the relief pattern of the carpet. At some point, I grip the edge of the bed and my legs begin to obey me again, my arms too, and once I have dragged myself into bed, once I have placed my head on the pillow, I feel strangely rested.

Then I get up. I organize my clothes in the wardrobe, set

my alarm clock, change the sheets, straighten the curtains, take a short walk, wash up the plate and fork left from dinner, and return indoors with a glass of water. After drinking it, I notice that the room smells good.

I switch off the lights and sit on the bed, my legs crossed. Placed on the table, the water glass looks like a piece of coral.

I don't sleep at all that night because I know precisely what I must do next, where to go, what to say.

Perhaps he exists after all. God.

*have you ever held a gun felt its weight in the palm of your hand, how
heavy and hot it is when it's fired*

*have you ever told a patient you'll be fine knowing they won't be fine,
pumped them full of sedatives in vain watched from the sidelines as
they die*

*have you ever dreamed of the devil—how he rises from the shore
and walks toward you and lies down next to you beneath the same*

parasol—a dream so real that in the morning you thought he was
breathing against your face and didn't dare open your eyes

have you ever said I love you though you didn't mean it

have you ever been in war have you ever kil

Have you

I have

13

I leave on Sunday. I buy myself a camera, a recorder, and a leather briefcase, I put on the only suit I own and rent an SUV; it's all very expensive.

As I drive out of the city, I realize I've spent my entire life waiting. Some people are like that. They wait, walk from one room to the next and wait, they cry and wait, sit in armchairs and wait, they wait to get married, they wait to become a parent, wait for their children to graduate and enter a profession, they wait for food to be ready, for the weekend to come, to get more money for their work.

Then there are those who don't wait but who act, those who ask and shall then receive, those who do not know what waiting is, those who graduate from school, form couples, have children, and work endlessly and take what belongs to them.

I will not wait another moment, I repeat to myself, I put my foot on the gas and refuse to be afraid. I will take it, I tell myself out loud, I will take it, once and for all I will take back what was taken from me.

I pass countless houses that all look the same, many of them erected right at the side of the road. The ground floor of these two-, three-, and four-story houses is almost invariably a retail space, a show of the owner's long-dead dreams, evidence of a father who never managed to get his business off the ground, a son who realized there's no point having a shop in the middle of nowhere, took his family, and moved to the city. It was only after I left Kosovo that I started to question the Albanians' constant urge to start family businesses, and while I was away I realized how little sense it makes, because you can't open something in every house, and certainly not a business that will be profitable.

The windows and balconies face the road, because preferably you shouldn't be able to see into the neighbors' yard from your own house, and the girls and young women hanging out washing on the balconies make me feel sad, the way they stare at the passing cars as if hoping that one of them might stop outside their house and take them away. They all have the same expression that you can make out from a distance, the same supine body language, their face stiff, their gaze hollow like someone who is about to lose their mind in the melting ennui of passing time.

Though the hospital isn't far from Pristina, the journey takes several hours because the roads are terrible. I park the car in front of the hospital's rusty gates, step out, and with the camera dangling from my neck, I begin ostentatiously taking photographs of the damp and cracked building with small sash windows that resembles an army barracks. The brown lawn surrounding the decrepit walls makes the place look like a burned-out barn with an abandoned ship rising from inside.

I take pictures of the grimacing profiles that appear in the cracked window frames, of the surrounding forest, filtering a ghostly haze that hangs above the courtyard, of the barbed-wire perimeter fence separating the worlds of the living and the dead like the stone walls around a cemetery, of the yard covered in cigarette butts, empty save for a few wooden benches swollen from the rain.

Then they arrive. The guards and staff run out from behind the building; at first they politely ask me to leave, and when I refuse they threaten me. I tell them that I am a reporter and that I'd like to discuss some financial matters with the director of the hospital. Fifteen minutes later I am waiting in an office that looks like a police interview room with metal tables and filing cabinets. On the wall is a framed poster of Kosovan separatist hero Adem Jashari.

To my surprise, the hospital's director is a woman; she walks to the other side of the table, stony-faced. I have no doubt she has found herself in similar situations countless times before. She knows what she is doing, but she doesn't know that I know what I'm doing too, she is unaware that in my imagination I've already met her, already talked to her.

"What do you want?" she asks, sits down, and leans against the back of her chair, its worn-out wheels squeaking against the gray tiled floor.

I tell her why I am here, my voice remains calm and even, serious but dignified and confident; I articulate the words as clearly as I can, I make concrete suggestions and present my demands. I am not here to bargain.

My name is Mehmet Rugova.

I work for a large daily newspaper as a correspondent covering Balkan politics.

I've been sent here to write an article.

You make healthy people sick here.

God is great.

God can see far.

One of your patients is a man who has no business being here.

His name is Miloš Micić.

The paper's editorial board wants him out of here immediately.

He is involved in an important series of events about which we want to publish a story.

This is nonnegotiable. This man must be released forthwith.

Do you understand?

I implore you to cooperate.

In return, the paper is willing to make a donation to your hospital of five hundred euros.

The woman pulls a cigarette from her jacket pocket and presses it between her lips, and once she has taken a drag of smoke she glances at the ceiling, the floor, the walls, then stares at me until she stubs out her cigarette in an ashtray bearing the logo of a sports club. She stands up and leaves the room mumbling under her breath, and my legs feel as limp as boiled bell peppers, my hands as moist as freshly caught fish.

A moment later she returns to her spot behind the desk carrying a file.

"Who are you really?" she asks, taking a thick pile of papers from the file.

"I am a reporter," I answer, undeterred, and at that the woman begins laying the papers across the table.

"This patient is in a very bad condition," she says and takes a deep breath. "He's been here for years."

I exhale a bucketful of air.

"He hasn't spoken for a long time; we believe he doesn't truly remember the time before the hospital. Do you know who this man is, where he has come from?"

"No," I reply and press my trembling hand into my jacket pocket to feel the envelope and, inside it, the money; it's most of what I have left. "I don't know anything about this man," I continue in a hoarse, scratchy voice.

"And where are you planning to take him?"

"To Pristina," I say and clear my throat so loudly that the woman flinches.

"Pristina?"

"Yes, Pristina. They're expecting him there," I say.

"Who is expecting him?" she asks, raising another cigarette to her lips.

"That I don't know," I reply, upon which she takes an indifferent drag on the cigarette, leaves it dangling at the corner of her mouth, and starts leafing through the papers again.

"We can't let him out just like that," she says through the smoke. "Surely you understand how frightening the outside world can be to someone like him. He won't be able to cope. He needs round-the-clock care.

"Who will look after him there?" she continues, raises her eyes to look at me. "Who will make sure he eats and suchlike?"

"I can assure you he will be taken good care of. This man is a Serb, he is a doctor, I know that, and I know there are people who will look after him."

"I know perfectly well who he is," she snaps. "I've seen him every day, spoken to him. You can't simply turn up here making these kinds of demands. This is a hospital, these people cannot survive on their own. Do you understand that? These people need help," she says, now agitated.

For a moment she falls silent, and the extended quiet makes me so nervous that I can't think of anything to do but continue the conversation, though I know it would be best to stop talking because she wouldn't have gone to fetch a folder full of documents if she wasn't planning on showing them to me or giving them away.

"*Zojë,*" I begin. "I do understand. But, to be frank, I think anywhere would be better for him, for anyone, anywhere but here," I say calmly.

"Is that what you think? Is it really? What do you think it's like working here? Do you think this is easy, do you think anybody actually wants to come here to treat them? To feed them, hand out their medicine? Would you do it? Would you? Well?" she shouts and slams her hand on the table. "The vast majority of these people have been abandoned, their relatives don't pay a penny for their treatment here, many don't even know of their existence. So you've watched a few items on the news, poor child, you've read a couple of newspaper columns, and now you think you know what it's like in here. Don't make me laugh."

I feel sorry for her and I try to apologize, to assure her that I really do understand, but I'm too late, she gets in first and continues her tirade.

"It's easy to come here for a few hours and pass judgment once you've heard how they shout and cry, once you've seen what bad condition they are in, then say this is the worst place in the world. But it is me who keeps them alive. Me. With what little I have. Me alone, I am their mother and their father. All the others, the nurses, the cleaners, the doctors, they come here for a while, but they always leave, before long they always leave. Nobody else can bear this place or the patients."

"I'm sorry," I interject. "I don't know why I said what I said. You're absolutely right, I don't know anything about this place."

"No, you don't."

I can see her sorrow, see that it is my sorrow too, that her sorrow is in fact the sorrow of this entire country, I see how it travels with her everywhere she goes, it is there when she takes the house keys from her pocket, when she prepares a meal for her family, when she shakes the rugs, wipes the crumbs from the kitchen counters, and vacuums under the bed.

"Here, this is a donation to the hospital," I say and take the envelope from my jacket pocket, place it on the table, and press down with my forefinger.

"And these," I begin and with my left hand take out my wallet, open it up with my fingers, and pull out six fifty-euro bills. "I would like to give these to you," I continue, raise my finger from the envelope, and slide the bills inside.

"No, no, no."

"I insist. Please, take them. I want to give these to you, by way of thanks for all the work you've done."

"Well, thank you," the woman says, momentarily closes her eyes, and swallows. "Thank you," she repeats, opens her eyes, takes a deep breath, and replaces the papers in the folder, which she tucks under her arm.

She rolls her chair out from behind the desk and hands me the folder with both hands.

"This man was brought here in a very bad state," she explains and glances down at the envelope, which I have placed on top of the folder. "He was beaten up in Mitrovica, he had spent a long time in the hospital before coming here, he almost died from his injuries; because he is a Serb he was barely even examined properly."

I do my best to pretend that what she says doesn't have the slightest effect on me, that the words coming out of her mouth aren't human words about another human being.

"He eats very badly, always has. But he understands speech, some days better than others," she says and holds a lengthy pause during which I tense my arms, tense my face, my legs, my stomach muscles, my shoulders and back, my entire body feels like it is on fire. "And he is very timid, that's what he is, sensitive. And he likes . . . ," she continues slowly. "He likes writing."

She grips my upper arm, strokes it, her toughened fingertips feel like tires driving across my skin, even through my suit.

"At first he wrote quite a bit, in a little notebook we gave him, but nothing for the last few years. I don't normally read the texts the patients write, but I read his. I've read them many times over."

Again she pauses.

"You're not really a reporter," she states.

"What are you talking about?" I ask, and at this my stomach starts to ache and my lungs begin to tighten so much that the folder and envelope almost fall from my hands.

"You don't have to pretend," she says, leans over and begins stroking my thigh as if it were a piece of her own itching skin.

"I don't . . . I don't know what you're talking about," I say and pull away from her in my chair.

"A reporter with a foreign newspaper?" She smiles, and it reminds me of my mother.

I pull a tissue from my pocket and wipe away the sticky film of sweat that has spread across my neck.

"Let's go," she concludes.

"Here," I say and hand her the envelope I promised.

"Thank you," she replies, stands up, folds it, places it in her pocket, and nods to me as if asking for acceptance, permission to leave, to take me to him.

We arrive in a small waiting room smelling of ethanol and old socks, with white plastic chairs along both walls. On a glass table in front of them, an artificial plant has been displayed in a vase that is far too big for it. In the foyer there is a reception desk and three doors: one leading outside, another probably to the patients, and the third to the staff area.

"Wait here," the woman instructs me and disappears through the door behind the desk.

I sit down on one of the chairs, lower my gaze to my numb legs, and don't dare open the folder she has given me. It stings in my hands, burning me the longer I hold it.

My mind is filled with a horror I have never experienced before. The woman is going to take my money, I tell myself, everything she's said is a lie, he's not really here, I must have seen wrong. I feel the sudden urge to flee. I want to run outside, back to the car. I want to stay where I am. I want to stand up, to stretch my legs, to sit down again, grip the chair or the vase on the table and smash the Plexiglas, knock down the doors, go behind the desk and ransack the folders, the drawers, and filing cabinet, to pour kerosene all around the room and set the whole building ablaze. I am angry and ready to lash out. I get up, take a few steps, sit down again and feel how tired and weak I am, and furious too, and I stretch my legs in front of me. I can't breathe but then I breathe so much that my lungs hurt. I should stop smoking. I stand up, sit down, stand up again.

A long time passes before I hear a sound outside myself: a hefty piece of iron clanking against another, then a heavy handle turns, a set of twisted hinges squeal as though they will never learn to bear the weight placed upon them.

First I see the nurse, just a young girl; she holds the door open and gives me a modest smile.

And then I see him—at the end of a long, dark corridor, he walks slowly, guided by the director, her arm around him as she whispers words of encouragement in his ear, dragging his feet across the cracked floor, toward which his face—hidden from the light—is turned, as though weighed down by an infinite guilt. Dangling from his forefinger is a plastic bag, which he refuses to give up, as though it means everything to him. Through the thin plastic I can make out at least two different fabrics, the edge of a wallet, a belt buckle, a notebook, and some pens, and I don't know why I'm looking at these things and not at his face, why I see only his greasy hair, his ashen skin, his dirty stubble, the contours of his muscles and bones, seemingly random like a broken trellis, but not his eyes, or why I still feel the urge to run, not toward him, but in the opposite direction.

2 DECEMBER 1999—DR. SELMANI, ARBËR

Patient found battered near Mitrovica,
left shoulder dislocated, left knee broken,
unconscious upon discovery.

Transferred from Mitrovica hospital.

Speaks little, responsive.

Claims to be a doctor.

Serb.

General condition, weak. Excessively thin.

Next of kin, unknown.

Continuous nightmares, prescribed sedatives.

14

PRISTINA, 2004

He sits in the passenger seat next to me, motionless, and I try to
let out short coughs and pointed sighs simply to fill the silence.

I have imagined this moment, so many times and in so many
different ways: what I might think, what I'll do, the feel of his fingers against mine, how his scent and voice might have changed—
the two of us, so close to each other after all these years.

But in my imagination he was another man, not this emaciated, silent, and confused human form, devoid of senses and that
cannot be touched. He scares me somehow, with everything he
is and is not, with his stillness, his reluctance to speak, his terrible
smell, with his shaved head covered in scars, strips of dried skin,
and oozing blisters, with his skeletal fingers and wrists, his knob-
bly knees and shoulders that look so strange, like little clusters of

grapes, with his clavicle, the edges of which look like the prongs of a fork, even with the plastic bag in his lap.

He doesn't look like a living being whose body is a home for human thought and action, but an empty birdcage, an object forgotten in a closet, a broken clock, a toy in which the batteries have died.

Driving feels so difficult that I turn toward a gas station, which rises from the middle of the field like a rusty anchor from muddy water.

"Hey," I say and turn to look at him with a smile, and he flinches immediately, as though I have said too much in one go, too much and too eagerly.

"Are you hungry?" I ask, slowly, hoping he will look at me and see from my smile that everything is okay, everything will work out, that I will take care of everything.

He lowers his chin, pulls his shoulders even closer together, and from the way his eyeballs dart from side to side as though they want to jump out of their sockets, from the way his eyelids blink rapidly as though he were trying to get rid of a resilient piece of dirt, I can see that he is terrified.

I open the door, get out of the car, and step inside the gas station, the elderly woman behind the counter says something to me that I can't hear, and I fill my arms with potato chips, chocolate bars, candy, nuts, water, and soda, wondering whether I left the car doors unlocked because I didn't want to frighten him or because I hoped he would escape while I was shopping, that he would break into a run, that in the middle of the wilderness he would feel the fresh grass against the soles of his feet, the gentle, cool breeze against his skin as day turns to evening, and would end up on a high ledge where he could see far and wide, people in their homes, the lights of villages and cities and swaths of verdant trees, and then the rain that had been forecast that evening would wash him clean and he would be warm, he could stay there, he could let go.

I place my shopping by the register, and the woman starts packing the items into a plastic bag, and on the counter I notice a basket of fruit where, crowning the overripe bananas, the soft peaches, and black-spotted pears, there are two fresh, flawless green apples, their skins shiny. I pick them up too, put one in each pocket.

Back in the car I take the water bottle and offer it to him first, and I am not the least surprised that he doesn't appear to see it at all, neither am I surprised that he doesn't touch the bag of chips or the chocolates, nor the fact that he doesn't seem to hear me as I explain whatever it is I'm holding in my hand and where I'm going to put it, the water and the juice in the bottle holders behind the hand brake, then the nuts, they are on the back seat, along with the candies and other treats.

We set off again, the sky looks like slowly bubbling porridge, and after a while I slip my left hand into my pocket, pull out the apple, and look at it, turning it in my fingers in front of the steering wheel.

Then I take a bite, and he instantly turns his head, and from the corner of my eye I can see him surreptitiously lick his lips, I can almost feel the saliva gathering in his gaunt cheeks—and then, without looking at him, I move my left hand to the steering wheel, holding the bitten apple between my thumb and forefinger, and with my right I pull out the other one, for him, his own apple.

I haven't held it above the gearshift for long when he grabs it with both hands and pulls it swiftly from me like a treasured object. He nibbles off a piece of the apple, then starts cautiously chewing it, all the while holding his cheek as if his teeth were aching, and for the kilometers that follow I am sure that everything will work out for the best.

We don't say a word to each other before Pristina. We don't have to.

We arrive late in the evening. He looks so frightened of the city's flickering lights that again I start commenting on the life around us, what is happening and where and what will happen soon.

I tell him I will leave the car near the city center in an unpaved yard that the owner has decided to fence off and turn into a parking lot—people will do anything for money these days, I tell him; here too, money rules everything. Then we'll walk to the house, I say, I'm renting one of the rooms there; it's nothing special, the kitchen, shower, and toilet are all outside, it's a very modest setup, but doubtless better than the place you were before, I say as we stop at a pedestrian crossing where a noisy group of young men on the road startle him.

"I have a bed and a mattress with plenty of room to sleep," I tell him, and we continue on our way, we pass a few familiar government buildings, a mosque. "And I've even got a television, you can watch programs all day if you want, and there's a fast-food place nearby that's open round the clock, just like in the big European cities, if you get hungry in the middle of the night . . . I lived abroad for a while too . . . in a city far bigger than this . . . You wouldn't believe how high up people have built . . . or how many people can fit into such a small space, how many airplanes fly over a single city . . . You know?"

By the time we arrive at the gate, he has closed his eyes and appears calmer, in fact he looks positively relaxed now, so I carry on talking as I drive up to the hatch where a parking-lot attendant sits on duty like a policeman.

"But when I lived there, I realized . . . ," I say and stop the car for the duration of what I'm about to say next. "I realized that what most people dream of around here, of getting away, of a new life in the West, it's completely different from how they imagine it. Because you know nothing about the life you are about to start, and nobody values the life you have left behind, after a while you won't either . . . Soon you won't even remember it . . . And then you forget who you are, who your children are, you don't know what significance your work holds or where your wife spends her time, what language your family speaks, with you or with other people, how they behave around strangers . . ."

I'm not sure whether I mention these things simply to convince myself of something, to defuse my nervousness, or because I notice he is all the calmer for hearing my voice. He lets out a strange grunt, it sounds as though he is trying to dispel a bad memory through his nostrils, and then the parking-lot attendant appears in front of the car and whistles and shows me to the left; it was that man who scared him, not anything I said.

As I park the car, inertia floors me; I can't open the door, either his or my own. I don't want to talk to the attendant, give him money for the night's parking, then ask Miloš to get out of the car and walk to the house together—if I have to carry him, if he is unable to walk by himself, what will people say, I wonder, what will they think, who is this man, they'll ask, this poor thing.

Please say something, just one word, anything at all, I think before opening the door and doing everything I am afraid of; I hand the attendant some money, tell Miloš over my shoulder that we'll be at my place in no time, then I convince him to stand and start to walk, and soon we arrive at the house.

I instruct him in whispers. He is astonishingly docile, walking quietly behind me, pulling off his tattered leather shoes outside my room, just as I do, and stepping over the threshold with his right foot. He even allows me to take the plastic bag carrying all his worldly possessions and place it on the floor by the wall.

He walks up to the window, pulls the curtains back slightly, and for a moment sticks his nose almost tight against the windowpane as though he wanted to smell it, then lowers his slight body into a chair, and as his eyelids soon press shut I see something approaching a smile on his face, only for it to disappear the minute I switch on the lights, beneath which the sight of him— his pallid skin covered in long, faint hair, his limbs that move slowly like boats in a gentle swell—seems anything but real.

I spend the night on a mattress on the floor while he sleeps on the bed, only I don't sleep at all but lie awake until morning, unable to relax, to steady my breathing. I know he isn't asleep either, but simply lying still, waiting for the night to end, the end of anything. I can't get up to look at him because I'm afraid his eyes will be open, possessed, glowing blood crystals in the pitch-dark night.

I've taken a few days off work in order to get everything done, to return the car to the rental company, to show him around and tell him it's best to keep out of sight of the landlord, at least for the time being.

As soon as Behxhet has left for work, I say to him: *A lot of cars drive past here, but there's no need to be startled by them, or the sounds of the local kids either, it's best to stay indoors, even during the day, but you can always go for a walk, to the park opposite or the streets nearby, as long as you come back before dark. You can take any clothes and towels from the closet, just throw the dirty ones in the basket, I'll wash them later, there's food and drink outside, above the oven and in the refrigerator, my things are always on the left-hand side, don't take anything from the right, only the left, there's water in the mornings and the evenings, they usually switch it off at night and during the day, be sure to remember this when you go for a wash, and yes, I've bought you a toothbrush and some soap, they are over here, the lowest drawer of this chest is all for you, you can put your things in here.*

I'm not sure whether he hears me or not, whether he understands a word of what I'm saying, because he doesn't respond to anything. I learn that it is best to talk to him in short sentences, to which he reacts either by turning his head slightly, closing his eyes, or swallowing, and for a moment it's as though he understands, as though he nods or shapes his lips into an answer, but a second later he disappears again, as if dissolving in water.

Questions seem to distress him, phrases such as "do you understand" and "isn't it" are like punches in the gut. I think it's because they imply a reaction from him, they ask too much of him, force him to become an equal conversation partner whose words should have the kind of gravitas that his spirit no longer commands. It frustrates me, though I understand that he has been away for a long time and that we have been away from each other for even longer.

On the second night he falls asleep for a while, letting out painful groaning sounds and thrashing in his dreams, and I sleep for a while too. It feels good: to forget that he is here, even if only for a moment.

But the following day he still doesn't say a word to me, doesn't change his clothes, wash, brush his teeth, eat, or even drink much, and I can't do these things on his behalf. Everything seems to frighten him; if I switch on the television, he doesn't like it, doesn't like anything that could be considered normal.

It's impossible to talk to him about the past, because he is not present in the here and now. I don't know whether he remembers anything or whether I even believe he knows who I am, who it is here speaking to him.

I'm away from the house for hours at a time. I go for walks, wander around the shops; we don't fit in the same room. I can't think of anything else to say to him and don't have the strength to take responsibility for all the talking. With the exception of nighttime, the constant silence feels unbearable.

The following day I tell him I am going to work and that I'll be back late in the evening, that things are going to change from now. I have to work, every day, all this costs money, I tell him, this apartment costs money, food costs money, and just as I expect, he doesn't react in any way whatsoever but simply stands by the window watching the brightening morning. At the front door I finally bump into Behxhet, whom I decide to tell that my brother is visiting me, and that he is a bit ill, in the mind.

"Very well," Behxhet replies. "My condolences."

At work, I drive the bus along the familiar route from Vreshta through the city center to the hospital and back again. In the afternoon a woman resembling Ajshe gets on my bus with a baby, and later on there are boys and girls my children's age, pretty as ripe plums, and seeing them makes me miss my family. On the wall of one of the buildings a new piece of graffiti has appeared; I can't make out the text but there's a picture of President Rugova's face, his mouth taped shut, and some of the houses have been put up for sale again, either that or I haven't noticed them before.

During my shift I feel I have used up all the energy I have. All day I regret not taking more clothes with me, yet I still periodically take off the sweater I put on in the morning.

I am irritated. I blow the horn at other drivers for no reason, brake suddenly, almost wishing something would happen to someone when I do. I can barely see where I am supposed to drive people, the roads carrying the weight of endless traffic chaos on their shoulders.

What I once felt toward him is turning into something else. I'm not sure what the emotion is, but I could drive the bus into a wall, into another car, I could kill all the passengers and pedestrians if I wanted to. I can do whatever I want. It doesn't matter, it wouldn't mean anything.

After work, I buy two burgers, costing a euro each, and just before turning in to my own street, I throw one of them in the trash, then I feel stupid because I guess I bought the burgers in the hope that we'd eat them together, that we'd watch television or something.

Then I feel frustrated, not at the fact that we won't share a meal together but because I wasted money on a burger I threw away, though I could have saved it for myself and eaten it later. It's going to be a cold night. By nine in the evening the wind is stinging my legs like a swarm of jellyfish.

I don't greet him as I walk inside, I don't want to, either that or I'm unable to form words. There are none. There is only a smell, his smell, he is lying in bed beneath the blankets, his eyes fixed on the window flickering in turn with the shadows of people's footsteps and the lights of passing cars.

He has wet himself and defecated in the bed; in places the blanket is soaking wet, in others hardened with green-brown shit. I take the burger outside, wrap it in the bag with the preserves, the candies, and savory snacks that I bought for him. The pieces of fruit I leave where they are.

I go back into the room holding my breath, take my suitcases from above the wardrobe, and begin throwing my stuff into them, clothes and other things that the living skeleton on the bed hasn't touched—the folder I was given in the hospital, important papers, a few photographs of Ajshe and the children.

I don't look at him, but I know he isn't looking at me either, and it means the end of everything.

I open the door, take the notebook from his plastic bag, and stuff it in among the food, and walk a short distance; people are watching, I cross the street, someone asks if I need help carrying everything, and I check into a nearby hotel after which I pick up a roasted ear of corn from a nearby stall, which I gobble down outside with terrific speed, though I don't feel like eating.

It crosses my mind that I don't have much money left, then I return to my hotel room and take a bath, I feel dirty, I scrub the backs of my knees, in between my fingers and toes, my armpits and back, and immediately feel better.

I lie on the bed and turn on the television. On the news there's a story about a man who was sentenced for the murder of his wife because she had tried to run away from him. Justice was done, I tell myself, and switch off the television. I send my boss a text message telling him I have stomach pain and can't come into work tomorrow. I sit up on the edge of the bed, then walk around the room a few times, take out the folder and his notebook, place them on the desk in the corner of the room, and switch on the reading lamp.

There they are, the countless reports from the medical staff, endless prescriptions, and treatment plans. Then his papers, his journal, all the lies contained within them. A whole world in a few dozen pages, some of which look like they were written by a child who has just learned to read.

I gather the treats I have bought on the table. I read one entry, eating my burger, then read another and eat a bag of nuts, then a third and eat the chocolates, I read more and eat more, and half-way through it all I think it might have been better to leave this food for him because now I feel sick, but it's not an option any longer, just as it isn't possible that there will be anything left in the morning, either to read or to eat.

When I reach the end of the journal, I vomit.

I wipe my mouth on the corner of a towel, wash my face, stuff the empty wrappers and boxes into a plastic bag, and throw it out of the window. Then I brush my teeth and lie down.

Hours pass before I fall asleep to a thought: our lives should have ended that day, the last time we saw each other, it really would have been better for us not to see the next dawn.

15

In the morning I write another letter to Ajshe.

> *Hi,*
>
> *I'm writing to you because I can't not write. You all must think that I am a bad man. Maybe I am. Maybe I became one without noticing, maybe it crept up on me like cancer. And I hit, though I wasn't supposed to be a man who hits his family.*
>
> *I have done terrible things, things that I thought I'd learned from. But I didn't learn, instead I did them again. And again. And again. It's because I forgot the consequences of my previous actions, forgot what this guilt feels like, the regret, the shame.*
>
> *I wish as fervently as one can wish for anything that you would visit and I could see you all again, because not a day goes by when*

I don't think about you. But I understand how unreasonable a
demand this is, how heavy and inappropriate, and that's why I am
calling it a wish, specifically a wish. And I won't apologize, I won't
insult you by asking for forgiveness, because I know that a man this
shameful doesn't deserve it.

Isn't it strange how—again and again, as if to humiliate
themselves—people fool themselves into thinking they can get time
back somehow? How time only becomes important once it has passed?

A.

I slide the letter into my back pocket, leave my suitcases at the
hotel, and set off in search of another place to live. I pass Behxhet's house and throw the notebook over the gate; it slaps against
the concrete floor like an apostate's Quran.

I quickly find another room, not too far from the previous
one and not in much better condition. The house is built on a
mountainside and has three floors, the middle of which is a unit
entirely for me. It has everything I need: a bed, a wardrobe, a
desk and chair, a small fridge, a chest of drawers, one cooking
plate, a few dishes, and a small pot and pan to prepare food. On
the ground floor is a spacious garage and an empty business space.

The house is slightly farther from the city center, in the so-
called gypsy neighborhood, but now I have my own toilet—with
its own entrance—built beneath the front stairs leading up to the
third-floor terrace. I'll have to buy a pair of sandals for that. My
room used to be a storage space, and it is relatively dark, though
the view from the small window reaches thousands upon thousands of buildings, even parts of the downtown area, and so its
dimness doesn't bother me.

My new landlord lives in Sweden with his family, this is their
"summer house," he tells me as he shows me around; the first

time I spoke to him was only an hour ago after calling a number I noted down on my route earlier. His two teenage sons slouch impatiently in plastic chairs, headphones over their ears, almost as if they don't care at all about what is happening around them. They don't greet me, don't offer me their hands, as young men should to their elders, but the mother of the family is pretty as a butterfly.

Before long we are sitting at a table on the terrace, which feels much higher up than my room, though the difference is only a matter of meters. Now I can see almost the whole of Pristina, like a pile of loose bricks, an innumerable amount of unfinished red-roofed houses, new ones constantly appearing like a rash that spreads but never heals.

The wife offers us tea, the man chain-smokes while looking worried, and I tell him I too have lived abroad for a while. In France, I say. I don't know why I lie about it, or about the fact that I am not married and don't yet have children of my own. I suppose it's because I guess it's more sensible under the circumstances.

"My daughter studies French!" the man enthuses and calls his daughter, who then appears in the doorway carrying a compact of face powder.

Fortunately the girl is so shy that she doesn't speak a word to me but simply grins coyly and turns back inside as though she were uncomfortable at the sound of my awkward haw-hawing, which even to me sounds crazy.

"So, while you're staying here, I'd like you to keep an eye on the house," says the man.

"That's no problem, I guarantee you," I reply and try to force a more natural smile to my face, without much success.

"There's nothing valuable inside, only the modest sofa beds, some old crockery, a small television," he lists and invites me to walk around the interior with him. He stresses that there's no point buying anything expensive here; we stay here at most one month in the year, he says, back in Sweden we have a flat-screen television and the children each have a room of their own, we have a large apartment near the center of Stockholm, paid for by the government, in a district where the children go to good schools, learn Swedish and other foreign languages, English, French, German, whatever they choose.

"I'm sure it sounds wild to people here. But we've lived there for so long, almost twelve years, the children were little when we fled, the eldest was four and the youngest was only one year old, none of them has any memories from here," he explains so slowly and in such a quiet voice that I'm not sure whether to interpret it as a sign of familiarity or disappointment.

"Is everything clear?" he asks.

"Yes, thank you. Everything is fine. I will pay the rent on the first day of every month to your cousin who lives about ten houses from here."

"That's right. Fifty euros. Does that sound okay?"

"Yes. Would you mind if I sat up here on the terrace while you're away? That view is so beautiful."

"By all means," he replies jovially. "That's why I bought this house in the first place. I tell people I have the most spectacular view in all of Pristina."

I move in that same evening, and a few days before the family's departure the man changes the locks on the doors upstairs. As they are about to leave for the airport, I hear the elder son, speaking in a deliberately loud voice, talking to his father, who tries to hush him.

"Dad, are you sure about this? I don't like that man, he doesn't seem very trustworthy. What if he trashes the apartment, invites his friends over, lets them stay here and live a life of luxury at our expense?"

They argue about me, and it makes me sad because, compared to other places where I've lived, this is heaven and I would never betray their trust. And so the father knocks at my door, and as soon as I open it I tell him I heard what his son said, he is an intelligent young man, it's true that anything could happen, but I humbly ask you to trust me, I will look after this house as if it were my own, I swear I will, you can send your cousin to check up on things whenever you want, yes, anything could happen, anything is possible, but as long as I am here I will keep my eyes and ears open, and I will ask you if anything comes to mind and inform you if anything happens.

At this he takes me by the shoulder and offers me his hand, which I grip as firmly as he does mine, and when they finally leave, step into their taxi and drive off, I walk a few hundred meters down the dirt track to the road along which my route takes me. I buy some groceries, a new SIM card, and a stamp, which I stick to the envelope with the letter I wrote to Ajshe that morning. Inside the envelope I put a note with my new telephone number and take it to the post office.

That evening I make a pot of soup with tomato, onion, and paprika. I season it with *ajvar* and Vegeta and eat it with a fresh white roll that costs only ten cents at the bakery.

At night packs of stray dogs gather across the mountain, and they make a terrible racket, barking and howling in hunger. Where do they spend the day, I wonder, and I feel so bad for them that I take out some scraps. But when they come, they start fighting over the food, and one of the dogs bites another on the shoulder blade with such untrammeled rage that the loser runs away limping.

I try to shoo the dog that has brazenly claimed the food for itself by banging on the window and growling angrily from behind the glass, but the dog just growls back at me, its yellow teeth bared, trickles of thick, frothing spittle along its scarred muzzle. I haven't seen anything this menacing for a long time, and when the dog finally disappears I sigh with relief, try to calm my pulse and get to sleep, but the sight keeps me awake long into the night. A dog is a truly terrifying creature.

The following morning I take a hose and rinse the dried blood from the concrete and swear I will never leave food out again, I even apologize to the dog that got attacked and suffered so horribly. It makes me feel a little better. I didn't want that dog to get hurt; I only meant to do good.

A few weeks later, I receive a text message from Ajshe, and when I read what she has written, I want to smash the telephone against the wall.

Hello Arsim. I've talked to my children. They don't want to see you, they said they don't have a father, and I have no need or desire to correct them. You are right, you don't deserve forgiveness. But neither do you deserve us in your life, you don't deserve to feel such happiness, or any kind of joy. It's best if you don't write to us ever again, we are nothing anymore.

I spend my free time lying in bed, staring at the bare walls with dry, stinging eyes. It lasts for weeks; at times I agree with her—they are probably better off without me—and at other times I'm so angry that I can't find a moment's peace. Doesn't she understand that I did try my hardest, that I supported them for a good time? Doesn't that mean anything to her, isn't that something? That I helped take them to safety, that I took my share of the responsibility when they needed me the most? I took care of things, I worked hard, bought them stuff they couldn't live without, I visited the children's nurseries and schools, built up a life from nothing. Doesn't she realize that fleeing was scarier for me than for her? That the language they spoke there was as foreign to me as to our baby?

One evening I receive a call from an unknown number.

"Hello," she begins.

"Ajshe."

Then she informs me, all in the same breath, as though reading from a sheet of paper, that she wants to see me the next day, she tells me at what time and in which café we will meet.

"This is important; be there at one o'clock," she says and hangs up without giving me the chance to suggest another time, to tell her I'm actually at work and can't just take time off whenever I want.

Despite my agitation I manage to call my boss, a confused conversation in which I lie, telling him I have such an extreme toothache that I'm about to faint with pain and that I have to get the tooth extracted tomorrow.

"Okay then," he replies with a deep sigh. "But if these sudden absences persist, you don't need to come back. Is that clear?" he continues and hangs up.

That night it pours with rain. Water slaps the concrete like hands against young cheeks, and I cannot sleep. It's still drizzling in the morning, and the rain finally stops just before I have to leave. I put on a suit, self-assured, but when I arrive at the café well ahead of time and order a small macchiato, I think maybe I should have left the jacket at home as it's far too big for me; when I sit down it droops unflatteringly at the sides and the bulbous shoulder pads make me look like a box, which only increases my sense of awkwardness. It seems I have lost weight, because only a short while ago the suit didn't feel big at all.

I take off the jacket and fold it over the armrest, from which it falls to the moist ground. As I reach out to pick it up, I manage to knock the table, spilling my coffee. The waiters chat to one another as I dry my jacket and the table, then they chuckle, probably at me.

I have to wait for Ajshe for quite a while, but when she approaches behind my back, there is no mistaking her. I would recognize her cautious steps anywhere, at any time, and on any surface. She stops momentarily, presumably to look around, and I don't dare turn, and a moment later she continues walking in such a way that her steps now sound fainter, by the final three steps she is creeping, then almost sinking down into the chair opposite, places her bag in her lap, calls to the waiter, and orders herself a large macchiato.

I expected us to hug or at least shake hands after all that's happened, but perhaps this is easier for both of us. During the night I'd hoped she would bring the kids to our meeting, but at the same time I had prepared for not seeing them; perhaps this is best for them too. Sometimes it's better not to remember where you come from, who your father is.

Ajshe looks intimidating. She has wrapped her head in a white scarf, her all-black dress and long-sleeved sweater cover her body, and on her feet is a pair of smart ankle boots. She doesn't look like herself. Or maybe it's the other way around; now she really does look like herself, finally.

I'm unable to say anything, I can't look her in the eye. The waiter brings Ajshe's coffee, and it feels as though the whole world is observing us, knowing who we are, what we are, where we've come from. Once the waiter has gone, Ajshe digs into her bag, and then I glance at her eyes: they are no longer brown but blue, and when she slides the opened folder in front of me, full of papers in a foreign language, and a ballpoint pen, I no longer feel anything at all.

As Ajshe explains the matter in the tone and manner of a lawyer, her gaze remains fixed on the paperwork, where there are a number of green Post-it notes indicating lines below which I should put my signature. There is a frightful number of papers, and I don't bother listening to what she has to say about them, let alone to read them myself, but I assume they are about our marriage and the custody of our children.

I am not remotely bitter or angry about letting her bring up the children. I guess on some level I know and believe that she is a better parent than I could ever be, than I have ever been. And I am not jealous either, because I don't know and don't particularly care to know whether Ajshe wants to find another partner whom she could live with. Maybe not, because her shoulders simply couldn't bear the weight of such shame. But it wouldn't feel bad at all, in fact I wish her only the best, even though she wrote to me saying I don't deserve any kind of happiness.

Once I have signed the papers, she places the folder back into her bag and only now takes her first sip of coffee. At this point our eyes meet for the first time, almost by accident, and behind the blue irises I can make out her dark brown eyes, scorched with a mixture of pity and loathing.

When she asks the waiter for the bill and pulls out her thick purse, I let out my first word, and it is "No."

"No, absolutely not," I add, place my wallet on the table, and gesture to the waiter, who nods in our direction and a while later returns to our table rather confused, then in a flash Ajshe unclips her purse, takes out a coin, hands it to the waiter, and tells him to keep the change.

For a moment I can't seem to breathe properly. I should give her two euros, I think, but I know that she knows I haven't got any extra money, so it would be strange.

"Thank you," I manage to say, coughing, and I almost feel like adding that this is very inappropriate, that women don't pick up the check, to say it so loud that the waiters hear me, so that they don't think I'm a certain way, but I lose control of my body; my head feels heavy, my eyes moisten, my face starts to tremble like when, as a child, I was so nervous about something that I almost wet myself, and then the tears start to flow, and they are stubborn, force themselves out, run down the folds of my cheeks, drip onto the jacket in my lap, my trousers, the table, then Ajshe reaches into her bag and hands me a tissue, which in an instant is soaked through.

"I'm sorry," I hear her say, and as I look up at her I notice her eyes turning glassy too. "I regret writing to you when I was mad, because when you're upset you end up saying and doing all kinds of things," she adds and blows her nose, then pauses, glances up at the waiters, who are staring at us, and her gaze is so cold that they understand to look away. "Sometimes I still wish things had turned out differently . . . that you and . . . Well," she continues, takes a deep breath, again reaches into her bag, and pulls out an envelope, which she slides toward me across the table.

"This is for you," she says, clears her throat, and adjusts her scarf across her ears, and as she does so I see she is wearing the golden heart-shaped earrings, the ones I gave her on our wedding day.

Things are exactly as she said in her text message: we are nothing anymore, we barely know each other.

"Well, take care of yourself," she says eventually, like she would to a stranger who has fallen over in the street, who has staggered to their feet by themselves and assured her many times over that it was nothing.

Ajshe stands up and leaves in the direction she arrived, and her walking away from me—it is war. That's where we are, the two of us; every step she takes is a bullet, each one fired from farther away, and though we are no longer near each other, ever again, we are always connected, blasted together.

you know I once wrote to that whore of yours I followed you home
I slipped a piece of paper under the door do you know where your
husband is I wrote on it, do you know he spends his nights at my place,
in another man's bed, a MAN's bed, he doesn't want you the same way
he wants me, he doesn't love you and will never love you the same way
he loves me

  you fucking whore

16

PRISTINA, 2004–

In the envelope Ajshe gave me there is two thousand euros. I use it to buy a decent bed and some sheets, a secondhand computer, and a new television and coffee maker, and there's even a little to spare. Money makes me feel good, safe; I constantly put some aside, though I don't know what for.

I manage to come up with a study plan, and by sticking to it I should be able to graduate from the university in a year and a half, assuming the courses I completed years ago will still be accepted. I am happy and proud of this, because having a university education is no small accomplishment. I eagerly await the start of the new academic year, though sometimes I wonder whether I'm too old for school. But as I agree to reduce my working hours with my boss, who is approaching retirement, he simply says it's fantastic news that I will be able to complete my degree. He even congratulates me. "Imagine, a future writer driving my buses," he says with a chuckle. To many people, a little over thirty is still considered young.

I read a lot of books, and I know that one day I will start writing my own, there will come a day when I will tell the world my story, there will come a time when people will want to hear me, perhaps after I've gotten over the shame. It's this belief that keeps me alive.

Shortly before I graduate, I send a student magazine a story I have written bearing the title "The Girl and It." Soon afterward, the magazine's editor contacts me to express interest in my manuscript, but they want me to modify it first, quite a lot actually, they want me to delete sections that I think are vitally important. At first I am skeptical of their suggestions but eventually I agree to the changes they ask for because the desire to have my text published is greater than the need to hold on to things that others find superfluous.

After publication, a few of my classmates come up to me and tell me they liked my story. Eventually I cut the spread out of the magazine and frame it, and as I hang it on the wall, I realize I've never hung anything up before. It brings me pleasure every time I look at it. At the end of the text there is a short biography and a photograph of me, I don't look all that bad in it. On occasion I pick it up and hold it in my hands; it is something concrete, and nobody can take that away from me.

After graduating, I get a job at the post office. My job description involves compiling content for the post office's website, writing various instructions for the employees and customers, even some amount of customer service. The wages are good, about four hundred euros per month, and that's plenty for me, I have even been able to travel to the coast once or twice, to Ulcinj and Budva.

For the first few years, my landlord and his family visit every summer, staying a month or two at a time. Their children speak Swedish to one another, and though they appear to trust me— they even laugh at my jokes and sometimes call me *axhë,* uncle— it always feels as though they are speaking ill of me, as if they can see through me, all my flaws and imperfections, as if they know things about me that even I don't know.

They have lots of guests, whom they generally entertain on the patio. At those times I prefer not to keep the lights on or go to the bathroom, I pretend I'm not really there, because if they noticed me, I would have to look up to them, to wait for the landlord's permission to walk up the stairs and shake hands with strangers. There's something demeaning about it, I think. It's probably only in my mind, because some mornings the mother and father ask me to eat with them, they tell me stories about their life, their children and relatives, and they always finish by saying how much they appreciate my help looking after the house. Then I thank them and say it's no trouble at all, though at times it truly is a burden. Whenever it rains or snows, for instance, mud builds up behind the house and I have to wash it away. Although I'm glad to do physical work to balance out my own job, it's hard labor.

As the years pass, they visit Kosovo less and less. The children's Albanian deteriorates, and each time I see them the parents look more exhausted and seem less at home in their own house. They don't bother to fix broken tiles, floors, faucets, and doors, they let the insulation hang loose, they don't even seem to care about the rising damp in the building. As summer arrives, I notice that I actually hope they will visit, because I am so keen to see how they have changed again, what their children look like now, though I'm not particularly sad if they don't come.

I sometimes walk past my former rented room, though only rarely these days. I have seen him hunched outside the house, a cardboard cup and a scale on the pavement next to him—or at least, I think it's him, I can't say for sure. He is always wearing the same clothes, and sometimes Behxhet is with him, explaining something to him, sitting him down on an empty bottle crate or wrapping an old coat around him or lifting up the sign by the wall advertising five cents to weigh yourself. I've always wondered what kind of person ends up on the streets, what kind of person can live like that, from other people's pity. His kind.

I walk past on the other side of the street and look away. I don't know why I even go there, because I can't say I feel much guilt or a duty to help. In fact, I feel I have the right not to take responsibility. I can't say I know that man, merely that I know the man he might once have been, and even him I knew only superficially, for one brief summer. And I don't know the man who once knew a thing or two about that man, because he too no longer exists. Neither does what once happened between those two men, what they once had.

I'm not sad and I'm not afraid of anything, and life has ceased to be only waiting for catastrophe, a message that, when it arrives, destroys everything you have managed to put together between disasters. That is surely something.

*I fought in Prekaz and Drenica and Rahovec and Račak, I was
everywhere and I remember all of it, all the details, the way the cattle
howled as they suffocated in the smoke, the way the ground shook from
the explosions, how long our ears rang afterward, which terrain we laid
with mines . . . how we pillaged and destroyed . . . and . . . hunted and
separated . . . who was raped and murdered . . . mercilessly.*

*I was in Belgrade during the air strikes, I was needed there all
through March and April and May and even into June, planes
flew across the sky like dazzling flashes, their missiles falling
indiscriminately like lightning, blindly hurtling on top of people, they
were slaughtering us . . . godless, for months . . . and there was this*

blown-up factory, nothing has smelled like the stench of the chemicals that rose up from there, it wasn't from the world of the living . . .

When a comrade asked me what else they will do to us in this hell, I remembered the night you read me the story you'd written about the snake and the girl, the night we talked about paradise and the devil who turned the baby girl into a bolla that would eventually turn into something even more magnificent, do you remember that night that creature?

I couldn't get that snake out of my mind for a long time, it lived in my thoughts all through the war and when we surrendered and when Milošević pulled the troops out of Kosovo, when I stepped through the rubble in Belgrade, like crossing a lava field, and even after the war when I returned to school in Mitrovica, where every day I walked along the banks of the Ibër, a river that had carried countless fallen. The sad bridge across the river separated the Serbs in the north and the Albanians in the south, they were still killing one another, can you believe it, death after all that death.

I thought about it and I thought about you as I walked there, always, I looked at the waters thick with ash, waters that had extinguished eternal fires, and I cried and asked myself whether you were happy with your wife and children, and one day I said yes, yes you are, it's a good thing you got away from here, I said again and let go, sent us flying like two birds that have crashed into the window, threw two smooth stones into the current

and I did not say sorry I said thank you

. . .

I don't think of those fables with fear anymore but as expressions of happiness, for one day every year it can flare, liberated and carefree, for a single day . . . it can fly unshackled above the waters and the forests, intone its grand melody in peace, stretch out its frame across the fields, the hills, and the mountainsides, hide above the clouds or with its wings cast enormous strips of shadow like starless nights, moisten its dazzling, shiny velvet skin in the lakes and rivers, fall asleep on stones and boulders parched by the sun, in the searing sunshine it can wrap itself around the trunks of trees or shelter from the rain by hiding beneath the leafy armor of age-old oak trees, and at nightfall it can slither back into its cave where it will lie, exhausted by that speck of freedom—one happy day is enough for it,

because the land it then inhabits, you see, it is the land of kings

Acknowledgments

To my trusted friends Merdiana Beqiri, Johannes Id, Päivi Isosaari, Jarno Kettunen, Aura Pursiainen, and Sanni Surkka. Thank you for all the insightful comments.

Sarah Chalfant, Sarah Watling, and Jacqueline Ko, who work so tirelessly on behalf of my novels. Thank you.

Thank you to my family for your support, wisdom, understanding, and the stories that inspire me to this day.

Thank you, Paavo Kääriäinen.

Thank you, David Hackston, for translating my work with such passion and commitment. Thank you to my wonderful editor, Tim O'Connell at Pantheon Books, for publishing my work in English, for the effort and dedication you have put into this novel. Thank you to all the fantastic people at Pantheon Books: publisher Lisa Lucas, publicist Rose Cronin-Jackman, and graphic designer Emily Mahon, as well as

Catherine Courtade, Altie Karper, Anna Knighton, Zachary Lutz, Rita Madrigal, Matthew Sciarappa, and Rob Shapiro, for the care you have given this book.

I would like to thank my home publisher Otava in Finland for bringing this novel to the readers. Jenni Heiti, Leenastiina Kakko, Mirella Mäkilä, Maija Norvasto, Silka Raatikainen, Kirsi Tähjänjoki—thank you. Once again, the greatest thanks go to my editors. Thank you Antti Kasper, Salla Pulli, and Lotta Sonninen.

Pajtim Statovci
April 2019